Information Theory: A Concise Introduction

Stefan Hollos and J. Richard Hollos

Information Theory: A Concise Introduction
by Stefan Hollos and J. Richard Hollos
Paper ISBN: 978-1-887187-28-2
Ebook ISBN: 978-1-887187-29-9
Library of Congress Control Number: 2015907737

Abrazol Publishing

an imprint of Exstrom Laboratories LLC
662 Nelson Park Drive, Longmont, CO 80503-7674 U.S.A.

Contents

PREFACE

Books on information theory tend to fall into one of two extreme categories. There are large academic textbooks that cover the subject with great depth and rigor. Probably the best known of these is the book by Cover and Thomas. At the other extreme are the popular books such as the ones by Pierce and Gleick. They provide a very superficial introduction to the subject, enough to engage in cocktail party conversation but little else. This book attempts to bridge these two extremes.

This book is written for someone who is at least semi-mathematically literate and wants a concise introduction to some of the major concepts in information theory. The level of mathematics needed is very elementary. A rudimentary grasp of logarithms, probability, and basic algebra is all that is required. Two chapters at the end of the book provide a review of everything the reader needs to know about logarithms and discrete probability to get the most out of the book. Very little attention is given to mathematical proof. Instead we try to present the results in a way that makes them almost obvious or at least plausible.

We start in the introduction with a discussion of how information theory has its roots in the field of communication systems design. This leads to the question of how to quantify information and how a logarithmic measure is the most sensible. The concept of entropy is introduced at this point but only for the case where all messages are equally probable. The introduction ends with two examples of how information concepts come up in areas seemingly unrelated to communication. The first is a number guessing game and the second is the problem of finding a counterfeit coin.

The next chapter looks at the problem of encoding messages as efficiently as possible. This is the source coding or data compression problem. The idea of prefix free codes and the Kraft-McMillan inequality are introduced. It is shown how the entropy is a lower limit for the average length of a code word.

The following two chapters discuss specific coding techniques. The first is Huffman coding. Three detailed examples of constructing a Huffman code are worked out. Software for constructing Huffman codes can be found on the book's website:

http://www.abrazol.com/books/infotheory/

The next coding chapter discusses a powerful technique called arithmetic coding. This technique encodes a string of symbols as a single code word. For long strings of symbols it gets very close to the per symbol entropy.

There is a long chapter devoted just to the concept of entropy. How to calculate joint and conditional entropy is covered along with a detailed example of how to use them. There is a discussion of mutual information, what it means and how it is calculated. This is followed by a simple example of how to calculate the entropy of a Markov chain. The chapter ends with an elementary example using the principle of maximum entropy to infer a probability distribution.

Calculating the entropy of English is covered in the next chapter. It shows how to use the statistics of n-grams to get a series of increasingly accurate estimates for the entropy. It also shows how to use the statistics of words to estimate the entropy.

The next chapter covers channel capacity and the noisy channel coding theorem. It shows in general how to calculate channel capacity but only the capacity of a binary symmetric channel is worked out in detail. There is a brief discussion of the noisy channel coding theorem with no proofs. The chapter ends with an unusual example of the use of channel capacity in gambling and investing. This is called the Kelly gambling system.

The final chapter is a brief introduction to the topic of error correction or channel coding. Repetition codes, parity check codes, and Hamming codes are covered.

We hope this book is useful for someone looking for a fast introduction to most of the major topics in information theory. An introduction that is concise but not superficial.

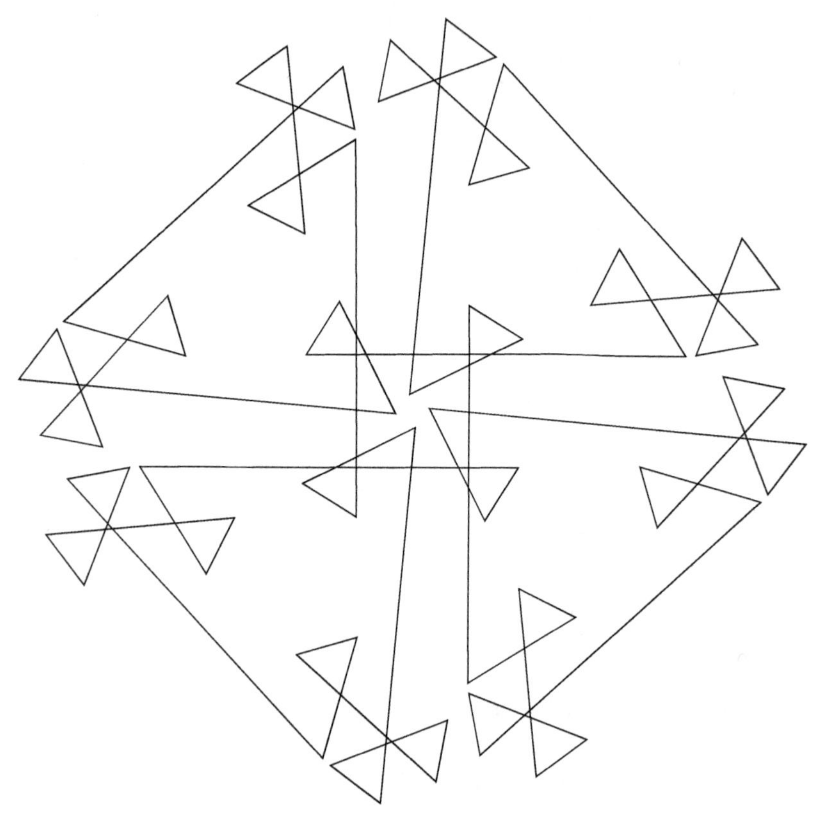

INTRODUCTION

The field of information theory was created almost entirely by one man, an American mathematician and engineer named Claude Elwood Shannon. This is a man whose list of intellectual accomplishments is so impressive, you have to wonder if he's not a figment of someone's imagination.

Figure 1: Claude Elwood Shannon, the father of information theory.

Shannon was born in 1916 in Michigan, and grew up in the small town of Gaylord, Michigan. In 1936 he graduated from the University of Michigan with a bachelor degree in mathematics and another in electrical engineering. He then went on to graduate school at the Massachusetts Institute of Technology. His 1937 master's thesis was on the use of Boolean algebra to design relay and switching circuits. This work provided the foundation for what would later become known as digital circuit design, which is the field of electrical engineering concerned with the design of digital computers and other kinds of digital circuits. His 1940 PhD thesis was on theoretical genetics.

After spending some time at the Institute for Advanced Study in Princeton, Shannon went to work at the Bell Telephone Labs. There he was exposed to problems in communication theory and cryptography which he worked on during World War II. In 1948 he published a paper in two parts in the Bell System Technical Journal titled "A Mathematical Theory of Communication". This paper is widely considered to be the founding document of information theory.

Shannon created information theory to solve communication problems. The goal of communication is to transmit information from one point in space/time to another point in space/time. Some common examples are radio broadcasts, the interaction of a web browser with a web server, and the storage of a file on disk for later access.

Communication problems fall roughly into two categories. First we have the source coding problem where the goal is to represent information as efficiently as possible. This is also known as data compression and it is widely used in computer and communication systems. Most image, audio, and video file formats use some form of data compression. The second category is called channel coding where the goal is to encode information so that it can be transmitted over a channel with as little probability of error as possible. Televisions, cell phones, the internet, CD's and DVD's all use some form of channel coding to reliably transmit information.

One of the first things information theory must do is provide a way to measure and encode information. In this chapter we will look at how to measure information and how the measurement is related to the way the information is encoded. The next chapter looks at the more general case where some messages in a communication system are more probable than others. Both this and the next three chapters address the source coding problem.

Measuring information mathematically, or objectively in any way, seems at first to be almost impossible. Humans attach differing degrees of importance to information. "Your hair is on fire" is generally regarded as more important than "you have ketchup on your nose". So how do you measure importance? Luckily we don't have to answer this question.

Shannon realized that any coherent and objective measurement of information must be independent of its importance or meaning. The only thing that matters is that information consists of a message or series of messages that are drawn from some set of possible messages. Some of these messages may be more probable than others. It is more probable that "you have ketchup on your nose" than "your hair is on fire". The probability of a message is what must be taken into account when measuring information. Information theory does not consider the meaning or importance of a message.[1]

Since this book is an introductory treatment of information theory, we will only consider the case where the number of possible messages in a communication system is finite. Suppose for example that there are only 4 possible messages. The messages could be something like: too much, just right, not enough, or no more please. To transmit a message simply number them from 0 to 3 and transmit the number. If the final recipient gets the number 2 then he/she knows it means "not enough". The communication system only has to deal with transmitting numbers. What the numbers

---

[1]Probability and importance are often correlated but this is irrelevant to the development of the theory.

mean depends on a predetermined agreement between sender and receiver.

This example suggests that one way to measure information is to use the number of possible messages. If each message is equally probable then getting 1 out of 16 possible messages provides more information than getting 1 out of 4.

To illustrate this, consider the problem of tracking grizzly bears in Alaska. Let's say that a particular bear usually confines himself to a 64 square mile area that is 8 by 8 miles as shown in figure 2. We want to monitor the bear's position. The figure shows that with 4 numbers his position can be located to within one of four 16 square mile areas but with 16 numbers he can be located to within one of sixteen 4 square mile areas. Clearly the 16 numbers provide more information.

While the number of possible messages is one way to measure information, a better way is to use the logarithm of the number of messages. There are several reasons for this.

First of all, consider the case where we have only one message. Is there any information being conveyed? Clearly the answer is no. With no alternatives, there is no information. We already know the bear is somewhere in the 64 square mile area, so the information is zero.

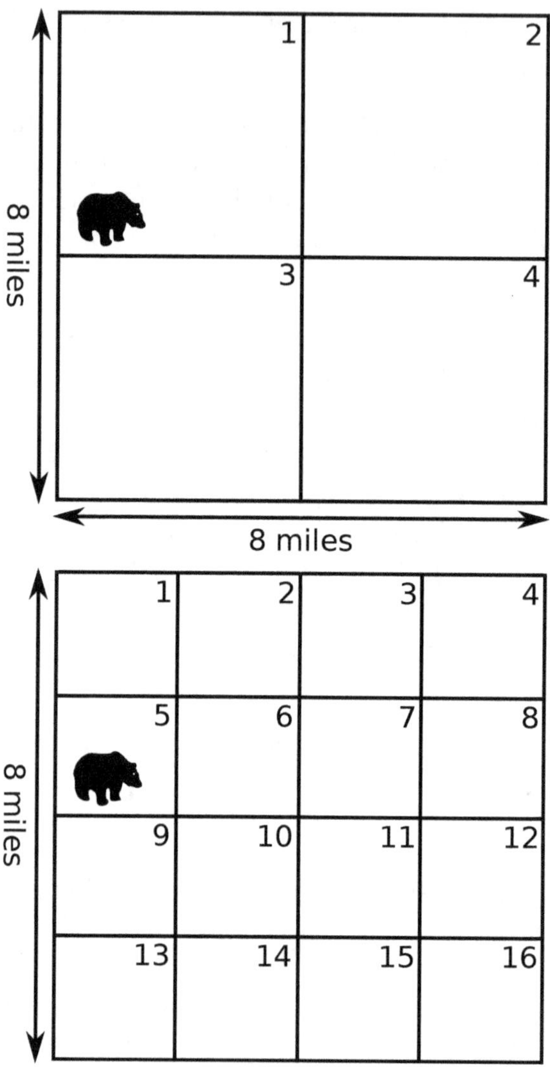

Figure 2: Grizzly bear tracking in Alaska.

How about if we try to measure the information content of more than one message? If the number of possible messages is N then there are N^2 possibilities for two messages, N^3 possibilities for three messages and so on. If we use the number of possibilities as a measure of information then we get an exponential increase.

It makes more sense to say that two messages provide twice the information of one message. The only function that is zero when $N = 1$ and increases linearly with the number of messages is the logarithm. We have $\log 1 = 0$ and $\log N^k = k \log N$. If $\log N$ is the amount of information produced by a single message, then k messages produce k times the amount of information.

The base of the logarithm is unimportant. The base plays the role of the units, in terms of which the information is measured, in the same way that inches, feet, and yards are units in which length is measured. In the same way that we can convert length measured in one unit to another unit, we can convert information measured in one base to another base. If the logarithm of N in base a is $\log_a N$ then the logarithm in base b will be

$$\log_b N = \frac{\log_a N}{\log_a b} \tag{1}$$

The base used will depend on mathematical convenience or on how the numbers in the communication system are represented and transmitted. A signal used to transmit numbers will usually have only a finite number of possible states. In the old telegraph systems, the voltage on the wire was switched between high and low values. Newer systems use techniques such as frequency shift keying where a sinusoidal signal switches between frequencies in some finite set.

It is common to use a signal with only two states so that the transmitted information is in the form of a binary code. The simplest way to transmit numbers in this case is to express them in binary form. The numbers 0 to 3 in binary are 00, 01, 10, 11. Each number is represented by 2 binary digits (bits).

Every additional bit allows twice as many messages to be transmitted. It takes 3 bits to transmit 8 messages, 4 bits to transmit 16 messages and so on. In general, you can find the number of bits needed by taking the base 2 logarithm of the number of messages. If N is the number of messages, then the number of bits is $\log_2 N$. The process of assigning a number to a message is called encoding the message.

Question: How many bits are needed to encode the 26 letters of the English alphabet along with the period, comma, colon, semicolon, left and right parentheses? Assume only lower case letters are used.

Answer: There are a total of 32 symbols that need to be encoded so the number of bits is $\log_2 32 = 5$. We could encode a as 00000, b as 00001, c as 00010, d as 00011 and so on.

Question: The ASCII character encoding scheme uses one 8 bit byte to encode characters (symbols). How many characters can it encode?

Answer: With 8 bits you can encode $2^8 = 256$ characters. The ASCII system encodes all the printable characters on a standard computer keyboard using the binary equivalent of the numbers 32 through 126. Numbers 0 through 31 are used for various control codes. The other numbers are used for symbols not usually found on a keyboard such as Greek letters, mathematical symbols, and smiley faces.

When information is measured in terms of the logarithm of the number of messages it is called entropy and is usually given the symbol H. The entropy in terms of bits is $H_2 = \log_2 N$. This is the number of bits required to send a message in binary code. To get the entropy in terms of decimal digits, use a base ten logarithm $H_{10} = \log_{10} N$. Entropy in base a can be converted to base b using $H_b = H_a / \log_a b$ where $H_a = \log_a N$ so that $H_b = \log_b N$.

Only when all N messages have the same probability is the entropy given by $H_a = \log_a N$. In general, the messages may have different probabilities and the entropy calculation must take that into account. We will see in the next chapter that messages with higher probability are encoded with a fewer number of bits than messages with lower probability. The entropy is then a lower limit on the average number of bits per message needed to encode a long string of messages.

Question: We have a communication system that transmits $N = 1024$ equally probable messages. What is the entropy in binary bits and decimal digits?

Answer: The entropy in bits is $H_2 = \log_2 1024 = 10$. The entropy in digits is $H_{10} = \log_{10} 1024 = 3.010\ldots$. Three decimal digits can only represent 1000 messages as the numbers 000 to 999. The minimum number of decimal digits is 4. The entropy in base b must be rounded up to the nearest integer to get the number of base b digits required.

Note that the entropy is often times not an integer. For example if N is not a power of 2 then $H_2 = \log_2 N$ will not be an integer. We said that H_2 is the number of bits required to transmit a message in binary code, but how can you have a fractional number of bits? The key is that H_2 is the average number of bits used to transmit not just one message but a string of messages. To better understand what this means we need to take a closer look at the problem of encoding messages which we will do in the next chapter.

Number Guessing Game

We finish this introduction by looking at some equivalent forms of the information transmission problem. We start with a guessing game played by Alice and Bob. Alice randomly selects an object from a set of N objects and Bob tries to guess the object by asking a series of yes or no questions. Since the objects can always be numbered from 0 to $N - 1$ this is equivalent to a binary search for a number from 0 to $N - 1$.

If $N = 8$ then Bob's first question should be "Is the number greater than 3?". If the answer is yes, Bob knows the number is in the set $\{4, 5, 6, 7\}$. If the answer is no, he knows it's in the set $\{0, 1, 2, 3\}$. One question has cut the size of the set that needs to be searched in half from 8 to 4. The next question can cut the size of the set in half again, and one more question is guaranteed to get the number. For $N = 8$ a series of $\log_2 8 = 3$ questions will always find the number. In general it will take $H_2 = \log_2 N$ questions to find the number.

This is illustrated by the binary tree in figure 3. The leaf nodes at the bottom of the tree represent the numbers 0 to 7. The root node at the top of the tree represents total ignorance. From there, we make our way down to the leaves by asking yes or no questions. A yes answer takes us down to the right, and a no down to the left. Encoding a yes as a 1 and a no as a 0 will turn the path from root to leaf into a binary representation of the number. This guessing game is entirely equivalent to the problem of efficiently encoding eight equally probable messages.

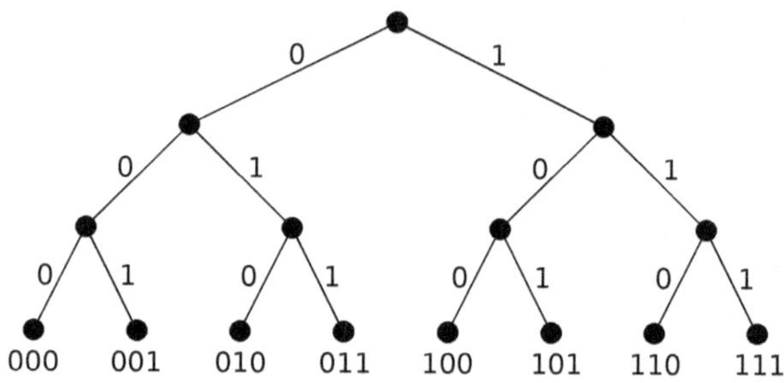

Figure 3: Binary tree for $N = 8$.

If we modify the rules of the game so that Alice can lie one time, then we have something akin to information transmission with the possibility of errors. Instead of messages, suppose there are two balls, one black and one white. Alice selects one of them and Bob tries to determine which one by asking yes/no questions. If Alice is allowed to lie once, how many questions does Bob have to ask? One method that will always work is for Bob to ask the same question three times. For example if Alice has selected the white ball and Bob asks the question "Is the ball white?" three times then at least two of three answers must be yes. If he asks the question "Is the ball black?" three times then at least two of three answers must be no. In any case, the majority of the three responses will be the correct answer to his question. This game is similar to using a repetition code for information transmission where each bit is simply repeated three times. A repetition code is used when there is the possibility that noise will cause an error in a transmitted bit. We will look at repetition codes in the chapter on error correction coding. For more on number guessing games, where lying is allowed, see the paper by Pelc listed in the references.

Counterfeit Coins

Another game involves finding one bad coin in a set of N coins. The coins all look identical but the bad coin weighs slightly less than the others. The only way to tell them apart is to measure them on a balance. What is the minimum number of measurements needed to find the bad coin?

In general the minimum number is the base 3 logarithm of N or $H_3 = \log_3 N$. To see why, let's look at the specific case of $N = 27 = 3^3$. Finding the bad coin will take a minimum of $\log_3 27 = 3$ measurements.

Start by dividing the coins into 3 piles of 9 coins each. Pick two of the piles and put them on the balance. If they are equal then the bad coin must be in the unmeasured pile. If one of them weighs less, then the bad coin must be in that pile. In either case the measurement will narrow the search down to 9 coins.

Divide the remaining coins up into 3 piles of 3 coins each and measure two of the piles. This will narrow the search down to 3 coins. One more measurement will get the bad coin. This is equivalent to encoding 27 messages using base 3 numbers.

There are many ways to generalize this game. We could for example consider the case where it is only known that the counterfeit coin has a different weight. It may weigh less or more than the other coins. The weighing procedure now becomes more complicated and it begins to resemble an error correction coding problem. Another generalization is to have two or more counterfeit coins. Many papers have been written on the counterfeit coin problem, see for example the paper by Guy and Nowakowski listed in the references.

ENCODING MESSAGES

Messages can be represented by numbers or symbols (letters of the alphabet for example). In any case they need to be encoded somehow. There is no loss in generality if we assume that a set of N messages is numbered from 0 to $N-1$. The problem then becomes one of encoding the numbers.

We start by looking at binary encoding. If $N = 2^m$ then each number can be represented by a unique m bit binary number. When all numbers (messages) are equally likely this is the optimal way to encode them.

When N is not a power of 2, things are only slightly more complicated. For example if $N = 5$ then 2 bits is not enough but 3 bits is too much. Three bits can encode eight messages (numbers 0 to 7) but we have only five. The solution is to encode some numbers with three bits and the others with two bits.

If the messages are equally likely then they can be encoded by assigning them to the leaves of a binary tree as shown in figure 4. The leaves are numbered from 0 to 4 and the corresponding binary code is shown. The number 0 is encoded as 000, 1 is encoded as 001, 2 becomes 01, 3 becomes 10, and 4 becomes 11.

The code for a leaf is found by following a path from the root of the tree to the leaf. At each node the path

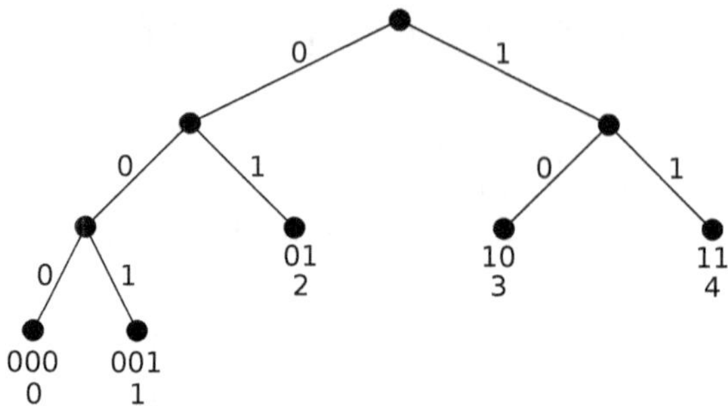

Figure 4: Binary tree for $N = 5$.

goes either right or left to the next node in the path. A step to the left is encoded with a 0 and a step to the right is encoded with a 1. Note that the code does not necessarily correspond to the binary representation of the number.

So with five possible messages we have two encoded with 3 bits and three encoded with 2 bits. Each message has a probability of $1/5 = 0.2$, so the average code length is $3(2/5) + 2(3/5) = 12/5 = 2.4$ bits. This is still somewhat larger than $\log_2 5 = 2.321928\ldots$ which we defined in the introduction as the information per message in units of bits for the case where all messages have the same probability.

The $\log_2 5$ measure is the lower limit on the average code length for encoding a string of messages. Suppose for example that we encode a string of three messages. The number of possible strings is $5^3 = 125$ and they can be encoded in at most seven bits since $2^7 = 128 > 125$. Using seven bits to encode each of the 125 strings will produce an average code length per message of $7/3 = 2.33\ldots$.

This is starting to get close to the value of $\log_2 5$ bits per message. We can get as close as we want by encoding longer strings of messages. To see this, note that we can always get a good rational approximation for $\log_2 5$ from its continued fraction expansion. A discussion for how to find rational approximations for logarithms can be found in the Review of Logarithms section at the end of the book. Suppose for example that we have a rational approximation a/b such that $\log_2 5 < a/b$ then $5^b < 2^a$. This means that a string of b messages can be encoded with at most a bits for an average code length of a/b bits per message.

Nonuniform Probabilities

Encoding messages that all have the same probability is easy. Things get a little more complicated when the messages have different probabilities. To analyze this case, let the set of messages be $S = \{s_1, s_2, \ldots, s_N\}$ and let the probability of getting message s_i be p_i. Assume that s_i is encoded by a binary string of length l_i, called the code word of s_i. The average length of a code word is then

$$\bar{L} = p_1 l_1 + p_2 l_2 + \cdots + p_N l_N \tag{2}$$

For efficient communication $\bar{L}$ needs to be made as small as possible. The probabilities are fixed so only the lengths can be changed. Messages with high probability should be given short code words, small l_i. Messages with low probability should be given long code words, large l_i. This is similar to what happens in human language where common words such as {I, me, a, one, the, or, and, but} are short while uncommon words such as antidisestablishmentarianism are long.

To minimize $\bar{L}$ we need to impose an additional constraint on what the code words can be. That constraint comes from the need to be able to decode a string of encoded messages. Suppose we have three messages $\{s_1, s_2, s_3\}$ with corresponding probabilities $\{0.4, 0.4, 0.2\}$. We could try to encode them as $s_1 \to 0$, $s_2 \to 1$, $s_3 \to 00$ but we run into a problem when decoding. Suppose we get the string 00. Is this two s_1's or a single s_3? There's no way to tell. Or how about 000? Is this three s_1's, s_1 followed by s_2, or s_2 followed by s_1?

To avoid this kind of problem we impose the condition that code words must be prefix free. This means no code word can be the prefix of another code word.[2] This kind of code is usually just called a prefix code instead of a prefix free code so that's the terminology we'll use.

It is clear that if all code words correspond to the leaves of a binary tree then the prefix free condition is satisfied automatically. A path from the root of the tree to a leaf will never pass through another leaf, so the code for one leaf can never be the prefix of the code for another leaf. This can be seen in the binary tree shown in figure 4. None of the binary codes that label the leaves are prefixes of any of the other binary codes.

Kraft-McMillan Inequality

The prefix free condition can be expressed mathematically as the Kraft-McMillan theorem. Instead of giving a formal proof of the theorem we will present it using a constructive approach. Let n_1 be the number of code words of length one. Since we are using a binary code $n_1 \leq 2$. The number of unused code words of length one is $2 - n_1$. Each of these can be used to create 2 length two code words so we have $n_2 \leq 2(2 - n_1)$ where n_2 is the number of length two code words. Likewise for length three code words we have $n_3 \leq 2(2 - n_1) - n_2)$.

---

[2]There are codes that are not prefix free that can be uniquely decoded but they are of no importance for our discussion.

We could continue on for longer length code words but let's keep it simple and suppose the longest code word has length three. Then we can arrange the last equation to get

$$\frac{n_1}{2} + \frac{n_2}{2^2} + \frac{n_3}{2^3} \leq 1 \tag{3}$$

This inequality must be satisfied by any prefix code that has a maximum word length of three. The way this inequality was constructed can easily be generalized to the case where the maximum code length is M. This gives us the Kraft-McMillan inequality. Any prefix code must satisfy this inequality

$$\frac{n_1}{2} + \frac{n_2}{2^2} + \cdots + \frac{n_M}{2^M} \leq 1 \tag{4}$$

The inequality can also be written so that there is one term for each of the individual code words as follows (n_1 of the l_i values will equal 1, n_2 of them will equal 2, and so on)

$$\frac{1}{2^{l_1}} + \frac{1}{2^{l_2}} + \cdots + \frac{1}{2^{l_N}} \leq 1 \tag{5}$$

where N is the total number of code words. Optimizing the code involves minimizing $\bar{L}$ given by equation 2 subject to this inequality.

Let's look at $l_i = -\log_2 p_i$ as one possible solution. In equation 5 we then have $1/2^{l_i} = p_i$ so the equation is satisfied as an equality, $p_1 + p_2 + \cdots + p_N = 1$. Equation 2 then becomes [3]

$$H = -p_1 \log p_1 - p_2 \log p_2 - \cdots - p_N \log p_N \tag{6}$$

where we have used H in place of $\bar{L}$. This is the entropy for the case of unequal message probabilities. Note that if all the probabilities are equal, $p_i = 1/N$ for all i, then equation 6 simplifies to $H = \log N$ which is consistent with what we identified previously as the entropy for all equal probabilities.

Average Code Word Length

As in the equal probability case, the entropy given by equation 6 is a lower limit on the average length of a code word. In some cases it may be possible to achieve the limit but in other cases it can only be approached as longer and longer strings of messages are encoded as single blocks.

To show that H is a lower limit suppose we set $l_i = -\log q_i$ for some value $0 < q_i < 1$ not necessarily equal

---

[3]From here on $\log x$ will mean the base 2 logarithm of x unless otherwise specified.

to p_i. To satisfy the inequality in equation 5 we must have

$$\sum_{i=1}^{N} q_i \leq 1 \tag{7}$$

The average code length is then

$$\bar{L} = -\sum_{i=1}^{N} p_i \log q_i \tag{8}$$

The difference between the entropy and this is

$$H - \bar{L} = \sum_{i=1}^{N} p_i \log \frac{q_i}{p_i} \tag{9}$$

Figure 5 shows a plot of $\log x$ and $x - 1$. It is clear from the figure that we always have $\log x \leq x - 1$. If $x = \frac{q_i}{p_i}$ then $\log \frac{q_i}{p_i} \leq \frac{q_i}{p_i} - 1$ and we get the following inequality

$$H - \bar{L} \leq \sum_{i=1}^{N} p_i(q_i/p_i - 1) = \sum_{i=1}^{N} q_i - 1 \leq 0 \tag{10}$$

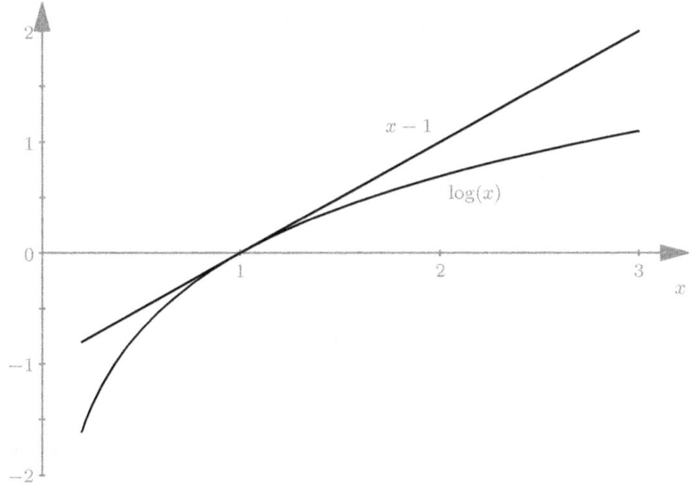

Figure 5: $\log x$ and $x - 1$.

From equation 7 we know that the last term in this equation must be less than or equal to zero which means that $H \leq \bar{L}$. So any choice of lengths other than $l_i = -\log p_i$, that also satisfy equation 5, will result in an average length greater than the entropy.

The problem with using $l_i = -\log_2 p_i$ is that l_i will only be an integer if p_i is an integer power of $1/2$. In general l_i will have to be the smallest integer such that $l_i \geq -\log_2 p_i$ or $l_i \leq 1 - \log_2 p_i$. The average code length will then always be within a value of 1 of the entropy. You can see this as follows

$$\bar{L} = \sum_{i=1}^{N} p_i l_i \leq \sum_{i=1}^{N} p_i(1 - \log_2 p_i) = 1 + H \qquad (11)$$

We have shown that the entropy as given by equation 6 is a lower limit on the average code length for a set of N messages with probabilities p_i, $i = 1, 2, \ldots, N$. The entropy of a set of messages is one of the most important concepts in information theory and we will look at its properties in more detail in a later chapter. In the next two chapters we will look at some practical methods for encoding messages. These methods can produce average code lengths very close to the entropy.

HUFFMAN CODING

Given a set of N symbols and their corresponding probabilities, Huffman coding will produce an optimal set of prefix free codes. They are optimal in the sense that the average code length is as close as possible to the entropy. The code was discovered in 1951 by David A. Huffman while taking a class in information theory at MIT. His professor, Robert Fano, one of the pioneers of information theory, gave the class the option of taking a final exam or doing a paper on finding optimal binary codes. Huffman chose to do the paper and discovered the method which he published in 1952.

Finding the Huffman code involves constructing a binary tree. We know that any prefix code can be represented by a binary tree where the codes give the paths from the root of the tree to the leaves and each leaf corresponds to one of the symbols being encoded. To construct the tree, start by creating a leaf for each of the symbols. Next, combine the two symbols with the smallest probability to create an internal node of the tree. Label the new node with the sum of the two leaf probabilities. Now combine the next two nodes with the smallest probabilities. These may be two leaves or a leaf and an internal node. Repeat this process until you get to the root of the tree which will have a probability equal to 1. We will show how this works in more detail with a few examples.

Example 1: Average Code Length Equals Entropy

In this example, the p_i's are all integer powers of 1/2. This will result in an average code length equal to the entropy. The symbols are $S = \{a, b, c\}$, with respective probabilities $P = \{\frac{1}{2}, \frac{1}{4}, \frac{1}{4}\}$. The symbols are sorted by probability, and the binary tree is constructed as shown in figure 6. The symbols b and c have lowest probability so we group them and create a parent node. This new node is assigned a probability of $\frac{1}{2}$. Next we group a with the parent of b and c and create a parent node for them. The parent has a probability of 1 so it becomes the root of the tree.

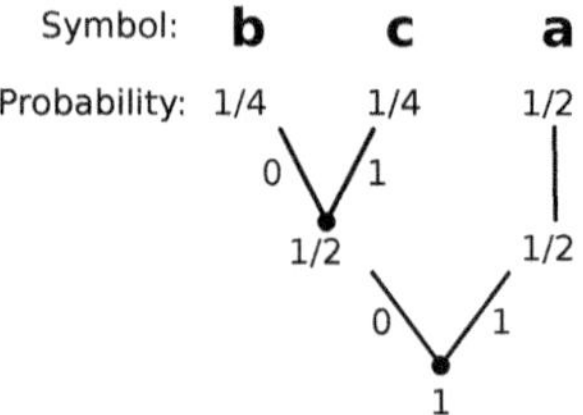

Figure 6: Constructing the Huffman tree for the symbols $\{a, b, c\}$ with probabilities $\{\frac{1}{2}, \frac{1}{4}, \frac{1}{4}\}$ respectively.

Cleaning up the tree and inverting it gives the customary form shown in figure 7. The codes are:

$$
\begin{aligned}
a &:= 1 \\
b &:= 00 \\
c &:= 01
\end{aligned}
$$

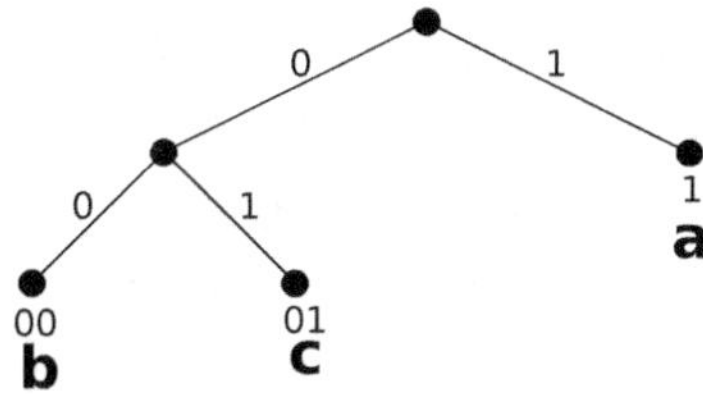

Figure 7: Finished binary tree for example of symbols $\{a, b, c\}$ with probabilities $\{\frac{1}{2}, \frac{1}{4}, \frac{1}{4}\}$ respectively.

Note that these codes are not necessarily unique. We could for example leave the parent node for b and c where it is, and put the node for a to the left of it. This would produce the following code:

$$a \;:=\; 0$$
$$b \;:=\; 10$$
$$c \;:=\; 11$$

As long as the topology of the tree is kept intact, the tree can be written in different ways to produce different but equivalent codes. In any case the average code length is given by

$$\bar{L} = 1(1/2) + 2(1/4) + 2(1/4) = 1.5$$

and the entropy is

$$H = -\frac{1}{2}\log\frac{1}{2} - \frac{1}{4}\log\frac{1}{4} - \frac{1}{4}\log\frac{1}{4} = 1.5$$

When all probabilities are integer powers of $1/2$, the average code length will always equal the entropy.

Example 2: Five Symbols Different Probabilities

The symbols are $S = \{a, b, c, d, e\}$, with respective probabilities $P = \{0.35, 0.25, 0.2, 0.15, 0.05\}$. The symbols are already sorted by probability, and the binary tree is constructed as shown in figure 8. The symbols d and e have the lowest probabilities so we group them first and create a parent node with probability 0.2. Now the two nodes with lowest probabilities are the newly created node and the symbol c. They are grouped to create a new node with probability 0.4. Symbols a and b now have the lowest probabilities so we group them to create a node with probability 0.6. There are now only two nodes left so we group them to create the root of the tree with probability 1.

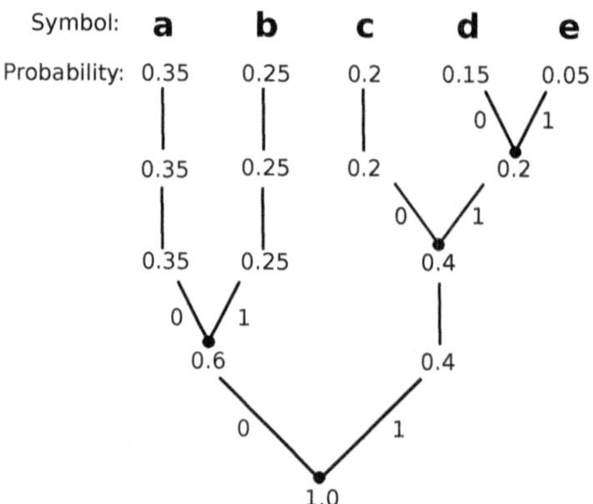

Figure 8: Constructing binary tree for example of five symbols with different probabilities.

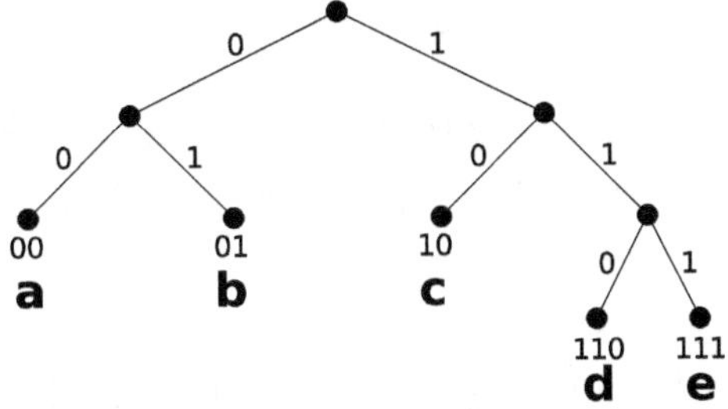

Figure 9: Finished binary tree for example of five symbols with different probabilities.

Cleaning up the tree and inverting it gives the customary form shown in figure 9. From the tree we see that the codes are:

$$
\begin{aligned}
a &:= 00 \\
b &:= 01 \\
c &:= 10 \\
d &:= 110 \\
e &:= 111
\end{aligned}
$$

As in the previous example, these codes are not unique. Rearranging the tree while keeping the topology intact will produce different codes but with the same length. The average code length is

$$\bar{L} = 0.35(2) + 0.25(2) + 0.2(2) + 0.15(3) + 0.05(3) = 2.2$$

and the entropy is

$$\begin{aligned} H &= -0.35\log 0.35 - 0.25\log 0.25 - 0.2\log 0.2 \\ &\quad -0.15\log 0.15 - 0.05\log 0.05 \\ &= 2.12112747\ldots \end{aligned}$$

Note the entropy is somewhat smaller than the average code length, agreeing with the fact that the entropy is a lower bound.

Example 3: Binomial Probability Distribution

If you toss n coins once or one coin n times, the probability that you get k heads is given by the binomial probability distribution:

$$P(k) = \binom{n}{k} p^k (1-p)^{n-k}$$

where p is the probability that a coin comes up heads, which for a fair coin is $p = 1/2$. We want to encode the number of heads that result from tossing four fair coins simultaneously, or equivalently, tossing one fair coin four times. The symbols to be encoded are the numbers $S = \{0, 1, 2, 3, 4\}$ and the probabilities are $P(k) = \frac{1}{16}\binom{4}{k}$ where $k = 0, 1, 2, 3, 4$. The symbols and their probabilities are shown in the following table.

Symbol:	0	1	2	3	4
Probability:	$\frac{1}{16}$	$\frac{4}{16}$	$\frac{6}{16}$	$\frac{4}{16}$	$\frac{1}{16}$

The symbols are sorted by probability, and the binary tree is constructed as shown in figure 10. As in the previous examples, the two lowest probabilities are grouped at each step to create the next node in the tree.

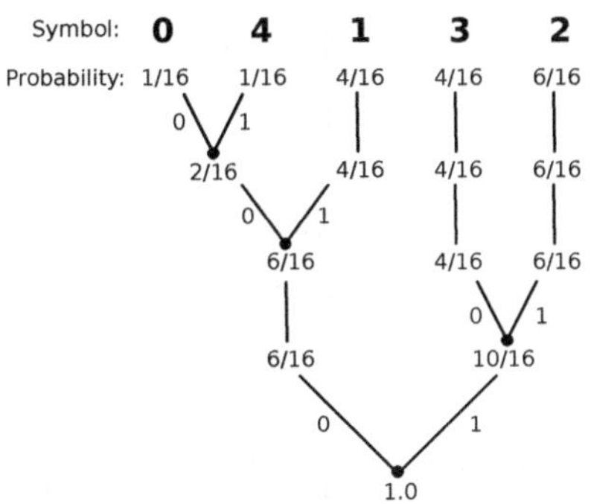

Figure 10: Constructing binary tree for number of heads when tossing four coins.

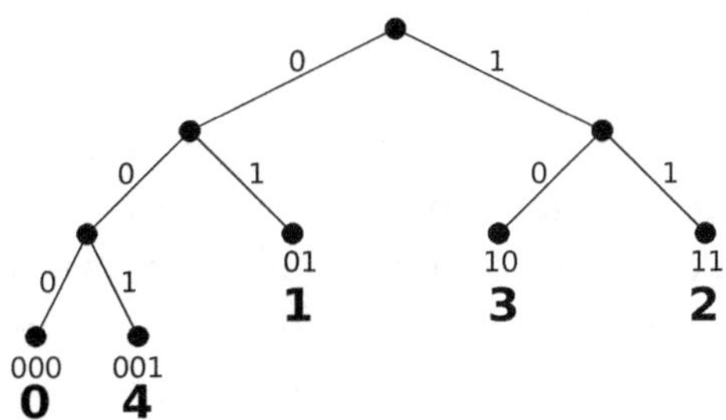

Figure 11: Finished binary tree for number of heads when tossing four coins.

The finished binary tree is shown in figure 11.

The codes are:

$$
\begin{aligned}
0 &:= 000 \\
1 &:= 01 \\
2 &:= 11 \\
3 &:= 10 \\
4 &:= 001
\end{aligned}
$$

Note that all the codes are shorter than the four bits necessary to record the result of four coin tosses. The average code length and the entropy are:

$$
\begin{aligned}
\bar{L} &= 3\frac{1}{16} + 3\frac{1}{16} + 2\frac{4}{16} + 2\frac{4}{16} + 2\frac{6}{16} \\
&= 2.125 \\
H &= -\frac{2}{16}\log\frac{1}{16} - \frac{8}{16}\log\frac{4}{16} - \frac{6}{16}\log\frac{6}{16} \\
&= 2.03063906\ldots
\end{aligned}
$$

The interesting thing to note about this example is that four fair coin tosses can be encoded with no fewer than four bits but here we have an entropy and average code length, for the number of heads in the four tosses, that are just a little over 2 bits. Somehow we lost almost 2 bits of information. Where did it go? The lost information is where exactly the heads occurred. In the case of tossing four coins simultaneously, which coins had the heads? In the case of tossing one coin four times, when did the heads occur? By encoding just the sum of the number of heads, this information was lost. This is an example of how you can get data compression by throwing away information, a technique that is used in common data compression methods such as the jpeg standard for compressing images.

Finding the Huffman code by hand is tedious and error prone for a large number of symbols. Luckily, it is not very difficult to write a computer program to do the calculation for you. On this book's website (http://www.abrazol.com/books/infotheory/) you can download a C program, called `huffman.c`, that will find the Huffman code given a set of symbols and their probabilities.

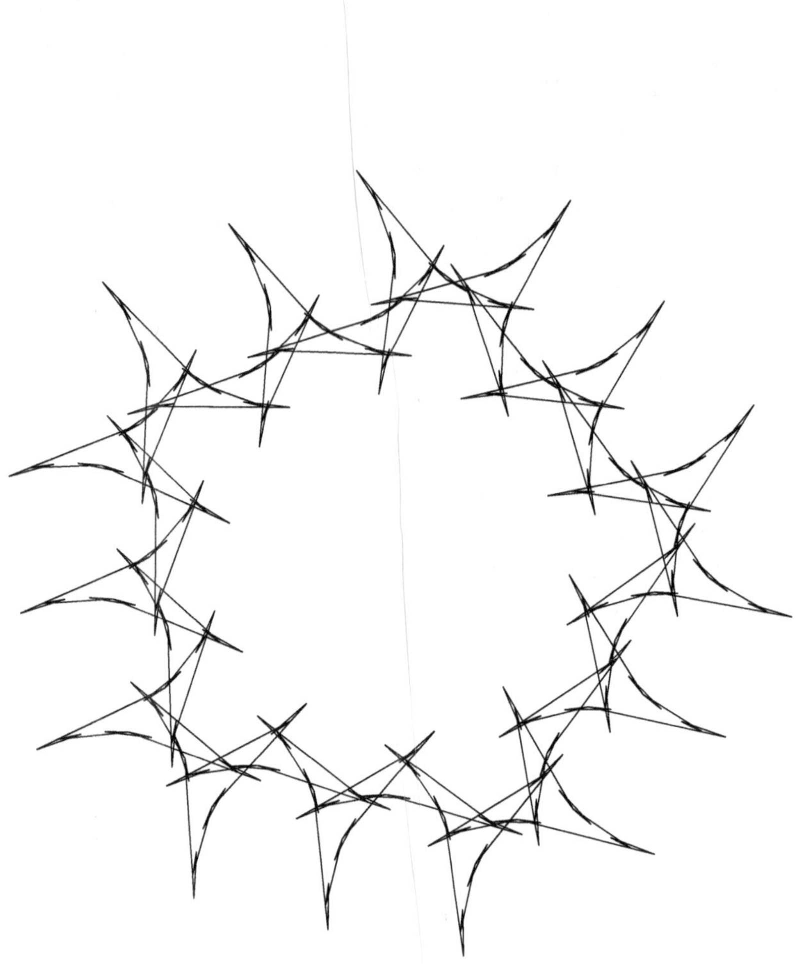

ARITHMETIC CODING

The idea behind arithmetic coding is simple. You map a message, composed of a string of symbols, to a subinterval of the unit interval $[0, 1)$. The mapping is done using the cumulative distribution of the symbol probabilities. The binary code word for the string is then the binary expansion of some number in the subinterval. The number is usually take to be the midpoint but it can be any point in the subinterval. It can be any point because every string maps to its own unique subinterval.

With probabilities that are not powers of $\frac{1}{2}$, arithmetic coding can be significantly better than Huffman coding. This is especially true when the message is composed of a very long string of symbols, such as a large block of text. In that case, arithmetic coding can produce an average number of bits per symbol that is very close to the value of the entropy. It achieves this by coding the entire string of symbols as a single block.

In theory, you could also do this with Huffman coding, but in practice it becomes impossible for long strings. Suppose for example that we want to encode a string of 100 symbols as a single block using Huffman coding. If there are 3 kinds of symbols then there are 3^{100} possible strings and we need to generate code words for all of them to get the code word for one particular string.

This is not just practically, but also physically impossible. With arithmetic coding it is possible to directly calculate the code word for one particular string of 100 symbols.

The best way to see how arithmetic coding works is with some examples.

Start with the first example we used for Huffman coding. We have the symbols $S = \{a, b, c\}$ with corresponding probabilities $P = \{\frac{1}{2}, \frac{1}{4}, \frac{1}{4}\}$. The symbols can be mapped to intervals in $[0, 1)$ using the cumulative probabilities: $f_0 = 0$, $f_1 = \frac{1}{2}$, $f_2 = \frac{1}{2} + \frac{1}{4} = \frac{3}{4}$, $f_3 = \frac{1}{2} + \frac{1}{4} + \frac{1}{4} = 1$. These partition the interval as shown in the following figure.

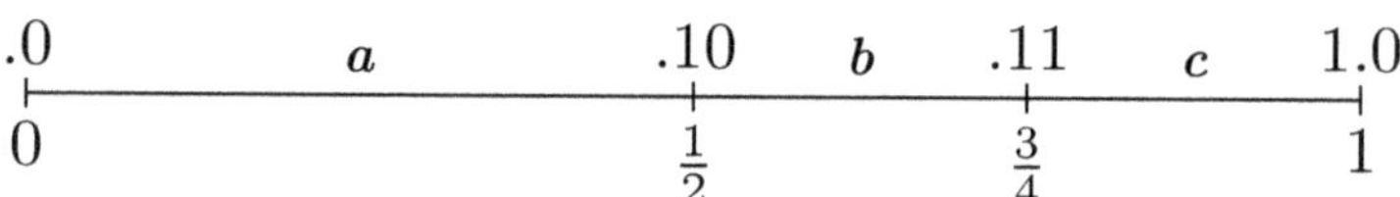

Figure 12: Example 1: partitioning interval $[0, 1)$

The symbol a is identified with the interval $[f_0, f_1)$, b with the interval $[f_1, f_2)$, and c with the interval $[f_2, f_3)$. To encode single symbols, one number is chosen in the symbols interval to represent it. In this example, if we choose the left end of the interval, we have:

$$
\begin{aligned}
a &:= f_0 = .0 \\
b &:= f_1 = \frac{1}{2} = .10 \\
c &:= f_2 = \frac{3}{4} = .11
\end{aligned}
\tag{12}
$$

where we have written the binary expansion of each f_i. We use $f_0 = .0$ because every binary number in the interval $[f_0, f_1)$ begins with .0. We use $f_1 = .10$ because every binary number in the interval $[f_1, f_2)$ begins with .10. We use $f_2 = .11$ because every binary number in the interval $[f_2, f_3)$ begins with .11. Note that if you take away the decimal point then you have the Huffman code for these symbols:

$$
\begin{aligned}
a &:= 0 \\
b &:= 10 \\
c &:= 11
\end{aligned}
\tag{13}
$$

In this case, arithmetic coding has given us essentially the same result as Huffman coding. The strength of arithmetic coding is only apparent when a long string (block) of symbols is encoded and the symbol probabilities are not equal to powers of $\frac{1}{2}$. Before moving on to the more general case, we will continue this example for blocks of length 2. Arithmetic coding will still have no advantage over Huffman coding but the example should shed more light on the two types of coding and how they are related.

Now we have 9 blocks of length 2. They are $S^{(2)} = \{aa, ab, ac, ba, bb, bc, ca, cb, cc\}$ with corresponding probabilities $P^{(2)} = \{\frac{1}{4}, \frac{1}{8}, \frac{1}{8}, \frac{1}{8}, \frac{1}{16}, \frac{1}{16}, \frac{1}{8}, \frac{1}{16}, \frac{1}{16}\}$. The cumulative distribution is $f_0 = 0$, $f_1 = \frac{1}{4}$, $f_2 = \frac{3}{8}$, $f_3 = \frac{1}{2}$, $f_4 = \frac{5}{8}$, $f_5 = \frac{11}{16}$, $f_6 = \frac{3}{4}$, $f_7 = \frac{7}{8}$, $f_8 = \frac{15}{16}$, $f_9 = 1$. These points partition the unit interval $[0, 1)$ as shown in the figure below.

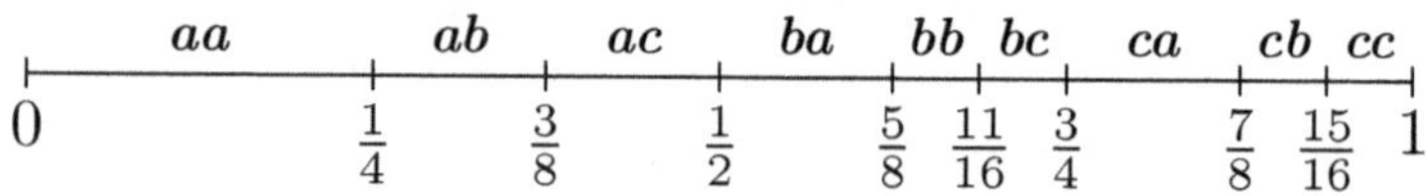

Figure 13: Example 2: partitioning interval $[0, 1)$

Note that you can get this partition by simply partitioning each interval in figure 12 in the same way as the whole $[0, 1)$ interval is partitioned. In other words, the first half of the interval for a becomes the interval for aa, the next quarter becomes the interval for ab, and the last quarter becomes the interval for ac and so on for the b and c intervals.

We identify each block with the left edge of its interval, so we have

$$
\begin{aligned}
aa &:= f_0 = .00 \\
ab &:= f_1 = .010 \\
ac &:= f_2 = .011 \\
ba &:= f_3 = .100 \\
bb &:= f_4 = .1010 \\
bc &:= f_5 = .1011 \\
ca &:= f_6 = .110 \\
cb &:= f_7 = .1110 \\
cc &:= f_8 = .1111
\end{aligned}
\tag{14}
$$

Now remove the decimal point and you have the code for the block. The code for aa is 00 because every binary number in the first interval begins with .00 and so on. Note that these codes are simply the concatenation of the Huffman codes for the individual symbols. This is because Huffman codes are ideal when the probabilities are a power of $\frac{1}{2}$. They produce an average code length equal to the entropy. They cannot be improved upon. To encode a string of these symbols you concatenate the codes for the individual symbols. There is no way to produce a shorter code.

When the probabilities are not a power of $\frac{1}{2}$ the Huffman code can not produce an average code length equal to the entropy unless very long strings of symbols are encoded. As the length of the strings increases, finding the Huffman code quickly becomes impossible. An arithmetic code can get very close to the entropy with long strings of symbols. It can do this because it only has to construct the code for the one particular string being encoded. We will show how this works with an example but first we need to lay some mathematical ground work.

From the previous example you may have gotten the impression that calculating the code for long strings involves calculating probability and cumulative distributions for such strings but fortunately this is not the case. It is possible to iteratively narrow down the interval corresponding to a particular string using only the probability and cumulative distributions for the individual symbols.

To see how this works we will simplify things and assume the symbols are just numbers (the actual symbols can always be numbered). The probability of getting the number i is p_i and the cumulative distribution is

$$f_n = \sum_{i=1}^{n} p_i \tag{15}$$

with $f_0 = 0$. f_n is the probability of getting a number less than or equal to n. For strings of numbers we impose the usual ordering where $nm < \acute{n}\acute{m}$ if $n < \acute{n}$ or $n = \acute{n}$ and $m < \acute{m}$. We then define a cumulative distribution on strings of two numbers as follows

$$f_{nm} = \sum_{ij \leq nm} p_{ij} \tag{16}$$

where p_{ij} is the probability of having the number i followed by the number j. Assuming only numbers 1 through N have nonzero probability, equation 16 can be written as

$$\begin{aligned} f_{nm} &= \sum_{i=1}^{n-1}\sum_{j=1}^{N} p_{ij} + \sum_{j=1}^{m} p_{nj} \\ &= \sum_{i=1}^{n-1} p_i + \sum_{j=1}^{m} p_{nj} \\ &= f_{n-1} + \sum_{j=1}^{m} p_{nj} \end{aligned} \tag{17}$$

If the numbers are produced independently so that $p_{nj} = p_n p_j$ then

$$\begin{aligned} f_{nm} &= f_{n-1} + p_n \sum_{j=1}^{m} p_j \\ &= f_{n-1} + p_n f_m \end{aligned} \tag{18}$$

or using the fact that $p_n = f_n - f_{n-1}$ we have

$$f_{nm} = f_{n-1} + (f_n - f_{n-1})f_m \tag{19}$$

We can use this equation to iteratively find the interval for strings of any length. To simplify the notation let the interval for a string of length k be defined as $[a_k, b_k)$. Now if the first number is n then $a_1 = f_{n-1}$ and $b_1 = f_n$. If the second number is m then:

$$
\begin{aligned}
a_2 &= a_1 + (b_1 - a_1)f_{m-1} \\
b_2 &= a_1 + (b_1 - a_1)f_m
\end{aligned}
\tag{20}
$$

If the third number is l then:

$$
\begin{aligned}
a_3 &= a_2 + (b_2 - a_2)f_{l-1} \\
b_3 &= a_2 + (b_2 - a_2)f_l
\end{aligned}
\tag{21}
$$

and in general, if the nth number is k then (note that the initial conditions for these equations are $a_0 = 0$ and $b_0 = 1$)

$$
\begin{aligned}
a_n &= a_{n-1} + (b_{n-1} - a_{n-1})f_{k-1} \\
b_n &= a_{n-1} + (b_{n-1} - a_{n-1})f_k
\end{aligned}
\tag{22}
$$

After the nth symbol has been processed, the code word for the string can be assigned to any point in the interval $[a_n, b_n)$. One possibility is to use the midpoint of the interval:

$$c_n = \frac{a_n + b_n}{2} \tag{23}$$

As we will see in the example below, the best point to use will depend on how the code word is to be represented, i.e. in binary, decimal or some other base.

Before we get to the example, let's look at how the length of the interval changes as new symbols are processed and how this relates to the entropy. Let $l_n = b_n - a_n$ be the length of the interval after the nth symbol has been processed, then from equation 22 we get:

$$l_n = l_{n-1}(f_k - f_{k-1}) = l_{n-1}p_k \tag{24}$$

Starting with $l_0 = 1$ we can recursively calculate the lengths

$$\begin{aligned}
l_1 &= P_1 \\
l_2 &= P_1 P_2 \\
l_3 &= P_1 P_2 P_3 \\
l_n &= P_1 P_2 \cdots P_n
\end{aligned} \tag{25}$$

where P_i is the probability of the ith symbol. Since $P_i < 1$ for all i it is clear that the length tends to zero as n increases. Suppose that after n symbols the number of i symbols is n_i then

$$l_n = p_1^{n_1} p_2^{n_2} \cdots p_N^{n_N} \tag{26}$$

Taking the log of l_n we get

$$\log l_n = n_1 \log p_1 + n_2 \log p_2 + \cdots + n_N \log p_N \tag{27}$$

Now divide this last equation by n and take the limit as n goes to infinity.

$$\lim_{n \to \infty} \frac{\log l_n}{n} = p_1 \log p_1 + p_2 \log p_2 + \cdots + p_N \log p_N \tag{28}$$

where we have used the fact that

$$\lim_{n \to \infty} \frac{n_i}{n} = p_i \tag{29}$$

The right hand side of equation 28 is the negative of the entropy so we have

$$H = -\lim_{n \to \infty} \frac{\log l_n}{n} \tag{30}$$

The number of bits needed to represent the interval in binary is $-\log l_n$. This is also equal to the number of bits in the code word. This result shows that the average number of bits per symbol approaches the value of the entropy as the length of the string increases.

As an example we will encode the string 12111, composed of the symbols 1 and 2, with probabilities $p_1 = 4/5 = 0.8$ and $p_2 = 1/5 = 0.2$. Start by calculating the cumulative distribution. We get $f_0 = 0$, $f_1 = 0.8$, and $f_2 = 1.0$. Next use equation 22 to narrow down to the interval for 12111 in a step by step process as the symbols are read. Start by setting $a_0 = 0$ and $b_0 = 1$. The first symbol is 1 which corresponds to the interval $[0, 0.8)$ and using equation 22 that is indeed what we get, $a_1 = 0$ and $b_1 = 0.8$. The second symbol is 2 so the next interval becomes

$$a_2 = a_1 + (b_1 - a_1)f_1 = 0.64$$
$$b_2 = a_1 + (b_1 - a_1)f_2 = 0.8$$

Continuing on with the other symbols, we get the values in table 1. The entire encoding process is shown in figure 14. As the symbols are read, each interval is shown scaled up to the size of the original interval and divided into left and right subintervals in the same way. The next interval becomes either the left or right subinterval depending on whether the next symbol is a 1 or a 2.

s	n	a_n	b_n
	0	0.0	1.0
1	1	0.0	0.8
2	2	0.64	0.8
1	3	0.64	0.768
1	4	0.64	0.7424
1	5	0.64	0.72192

Table 1: Intervals for encoding the string 12111.

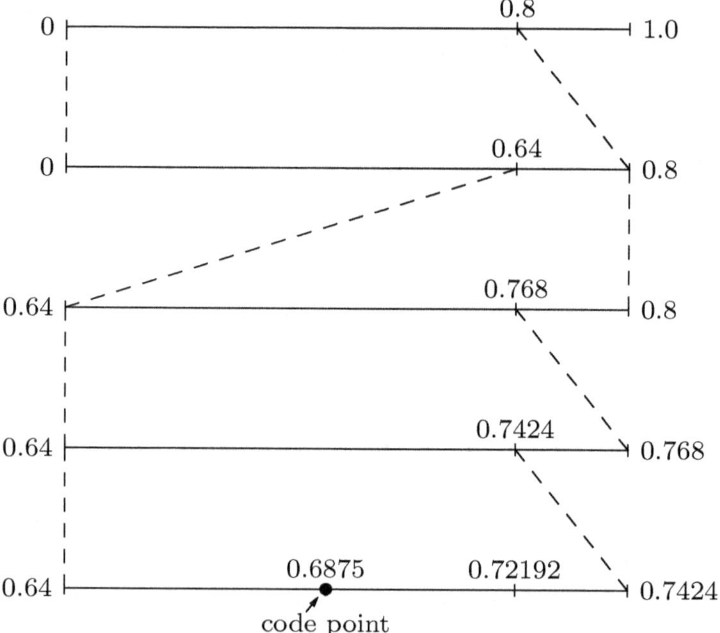

Figure 14: Coding example for the string 12111.

Once the entire 12111 string is read, the final interval is $[0.64, 0.72192)$. The code for the string must be a point in this interval. The best point to use depends on what kind of code we want. If we are going to use a binary code then we need to look at the binary expansion of the interval's end points.

$$0.64 \quad = \quad .101000111101011100001\ldots$$
$$0.72192 \quad = \quad .101110001100111110111\ldots$$

From the binary expansion, it is clear that $.1011 = 0.6875$ is a point inside the final interval. Removing the decimal point, we get 1011 as the arithmetic code for the string 12111. We have encoded the 5 symbol string 12111 using 4 bits. We noted above that the number of bits needed to represent an interval of length l_n should be $-\log l_n$. The length of our final interval is $0.72192 - 0.64 = 0.08192$. Taking the base 2 logarithm we get $-\log 0.08192 \approx 3.6$ which we round up to 4 to get the number of bits needed to represent the interval. This agrees with the 1011 code that we found.

Encoding is only half the fun. We still need to be able to decode to get the original string of symbols. The decoding process is very similar to the encoding process. Start by finding the code point that 1011 corresponds to, $c = .1011 = 0.6875$. To go from c back to the original string, we need a few additional pieces of information. We need to know the symbols, their probabilities and the length of the original string.

With the probabilities we reconstruct the cumulative distribution $f_0 = 0$, $f_1 = 0.8$, and $f_2 = 1.0$. Seeing that $f_0 < c < f_1$ we know that the first symbol must be 1. Now we basically follow the encoding procedure and narrow down the interval to $[0, 0.8)$ which is the second line in figure 14. From there we see that since $0.64 < c < 0.8$, the next symbol must be a 2. Continuing the process, we can reconstruct the original string. It is important to note that the length of the original string must be known, otherwise there is no way to know when to stop decoding.

There are a few problems that we glossed over in the description of the encoding and decoding process that make writing software, to do arithmetic coding, not as simple as it may seem at first. The biggest problem is that the interval $[a_k, b_k)$, corresponding to the data read up to the kth symbol, will continue to shrink as more data is read in. At some point the interval becomes so small that it cannot be represented with the standard floating point numbers available in most programming languages. Ways have been found to get around this problem. The best reference for a practical implementation of arithmetic coding is the paper by Witten, Neal and Cleary (see references). Their paper discusses an implementation of arithmetic coding written in the C programming language which you can download from the internet (see references).

ENTROPY

Entropy is one of the most important concepts in information theory and in this chapter we are going to take a closer look at it from a more mathematical point of view. In general we will consider a process whereby a series of symbols (messages) is being generated according to some statistical model, and ask how much information is being produced by the process. Such a process is called a discrete stochastic process.

In the simplest statistical model each symbol is produced independently, according to a fixed probability distribution. If $p(i)$ is the probability of the ith symbol and there are N symbols then the entropy, as we have defined it in previous chapters, is given by:

$$H = -\sum_{i=1}^{N} p(i) \log p(i) \qquad (31)$$

If all the probabilities are equal, so that $p(i) = 1/N$ for all i, then the entropy is simply the log of the number of symbols, $H = \log N$. When all probabilities are equal or nearly equal, the entropy is large. When one probability is much larger than the others, the entropy is small. This is easiest to see when there are only two symbols with probabilities p and $1 - p$. In that case the entropy is $H(p) = p \log p + (1-p) \log (1-p)$. This is called the binary entropy function and a plot of it is shown in figure 15.

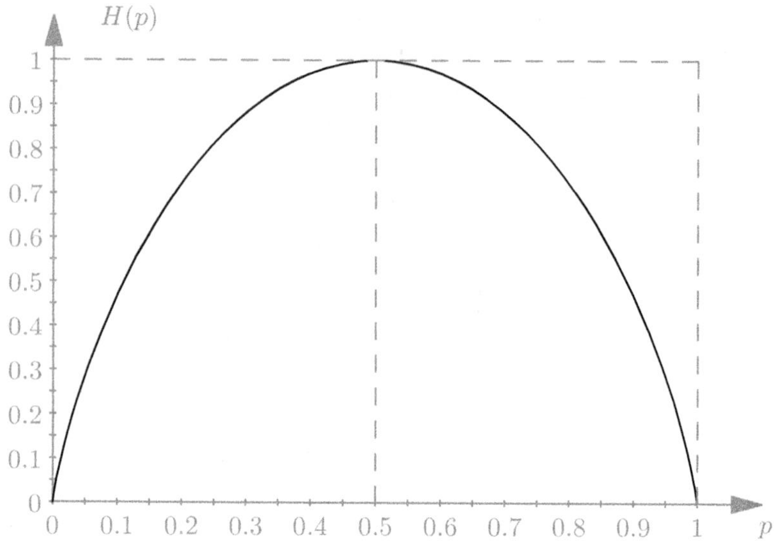

Figure 15: Binary entropy function $H(p) = p \log p + (1-p) \log (1-p)$.

The function has a maximum value of 1 at $p = 1/2$ where both symbols are equally likely. This means each symbol represents one bit of information, an equally likely yes or no answer. Near the ends of the range, at $p = 0$ and $p = 1$, one of the symbols is much more likely than the other and the entropy is close to zero. Exactly at the end points only one symbol occurs and the entropy is zero, meaning no information is being conveyed.

Now suppose we have two stochastic processes (message sources) and we want to measure their combined entropy. The first process emits one of N symbols which we will represent as the random variable X and the second process emits one of M symbols which we will represent as the random variable Y. We can simplify the notation a bit by assuming the symbols are the numbers 1 through N for X and 1 through M for Y.

Let $p(i)$ be the probability that $X = i$ and let $p(j)$ be the probability that $Y = j$. The joint probability that $X = i$ and $Y = j$ is $p(i,j)$.[4] The individual entropies of X and Y are then

$$H(X) = -\sum_{i=1}^{N} p(i) \log p(i) \tag{32}$$

$$H(Y) = -\sum_{j=1}^{M} p(j) \log p(j) \tag{33}$$

---

[4]To avoid ambiguity we could write these probabilities as $p_X(i)$, $p_Y(j)$, and $p_{X,Y}(i,j)$ but to avoid the cumbersome notation we will let the arguments i and j signify that the probability is that of X and Y respectively.

and the joint entropy of X and Y is

$$H(X,Y) = -\sum_{i=1}^{N}\sum_{j=1}^{M} p(i,j)\log p(i,j) \tag{34}$$

If X and Y are independent random variables then their joint distribution factors as $p(i,j) = p(i)p(j)$ and their joint entropy is

$$\begin{aligned} H(X,Y) &= -\sum_{i=1}^{N}\sum_{j=1}^{M} p(i)p(j)(\log p(i) + \log p(j)) \\ H(X,Y) &= H(X) + H(Y) \end{aligned} \tag{35}$$

For independent processes, the joint entropy is just the sum of the individual entropies. In general however, the joint entropy will be less than or equal to the sum of the individual entropies.

$$H(X,Y) \le H(X) + H(Y) \tag{36}$$

To see this, we write the difference as follows (expand the right hand side and you will see that the equality holds)

$$H(X)+H(Y)-H(X,Y) = -\sum_{i=1}^{N}\sum_{j=1}^{M} p(i,j) \log \frac{p(i)p(j)}{p(i,j)}$$

$$(37)$$

Using the inequality $\log x \leq x - 1$ with this last equation produces equation 36.

As an example of joint entropy, consider the problem of tracking a bear that we looked at in chapter 1. We divide the bear's range into quadrants as shown in figure 16. Assume he is equally likely to be in any of the quadrants so that $p(1) = p(2) = p(3) = p(4) = 1/4$. Let X be the random variable for the quadrant the bear is in, so that $X = 1, 2, 3, 4$ all with probability $1/4$.

In addition to his location, we get information about his elevation. If he is above 7000 feet his elevation is recorded as H (high) and if below 7000 feet it is recorded as L (low). Let Y be the random variable for his elevation so that $Y = H, L$.

To determine the probabilities for Y, note that each quadrant only has a certain percentage of terrain above 7000 feet and the bear is equally likely to be anywhere in a quadrant. Only 10% of the terrain in quadrants

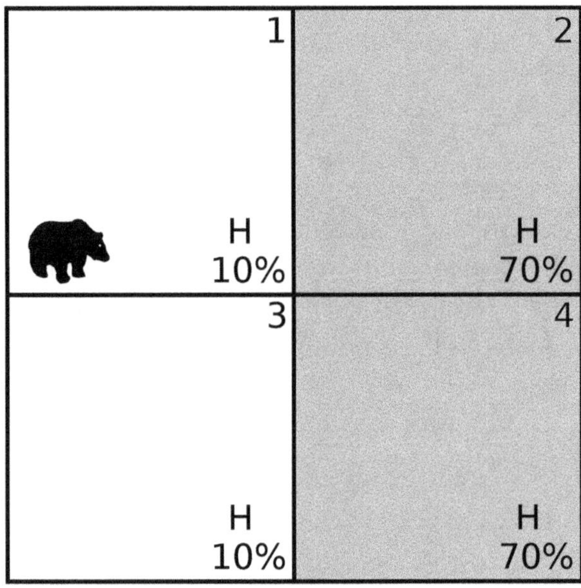

Figure 16: $p(1) = p(2) = p(3) = p(4) = 1/4$

1 and 3 is above 7000 feet, while in quadrants 2 and 4 the percentage is 70%. The conditional probabilities for Y given X, i.e. $p(Y|X)$, are then:

$$
\begin{aligned}
p(H|1) &= p(H|3) &= 0.1 \\
p(L|1) &= p(L|3) &= 0.9 \\
p(H|2) &= p(H|4) &= 0.7 \\
p(L|2) &= p(L|4) &= 0.3
\end{aligned}
\tag{38}
$$

From these conditional probabilities we can get the joint probabilities $p(X,Y) = p(Y|X)p(X)$.

$$
\begin{aligned}
p(1,H) &= p(3,H) = (0.1)(0.25) = 0.025 \\
p(1,L) &= p(3,L) = (0.9)(0.25) = 0.225 \\
p(2,H) &= p(4,H) = (0.7)(0.25) = 0.175 \\
p(2,L) &= p(4,L) = (0.3)(0.25) = 0.075
\end{aligned}
\tag{39}
$$

So the high and low probabilities are:

$$
\begin{aligned}
p(H) &= p(1,H) + p(2,H) + p(3,H) + p(4,H) \\
&= 0.4 \\
p(L) &= p(1,L) + p(2,L) + p(3,L) + p(4,L) \\
&= 0.6
\end{aligned}
\tag{40}
$$

Now we can calculate entropies. Since all quadrants are equally likely, the quadrant entropy is $H(X) = \log 4 = 2$. Using the H and L probabilities we just calculated, the elevation entropy is $H(Y) = -0.4 \log 0.4 - 0.6 \log 0.6 = 0.97095059$. The sum of the two entropies is $H(X) + H(Y) = 2.97095059$ while the joint entropy is

$$H(X,Y) = -\sum_X \sum_Y p(X,Y) \log p(X,Y) = 2.675143$$

$$(41)$$

The joint entropy is less than the sum of the individual entropies. This is because X and Y are not independent. Knowing the quadrant the bear is in changes the probability that he is at a low or high altitude. This means that encoding X and Y together, as a vector valued random variable $Z = (X,Y)$ with 8 possible values, will take, on average, fewer bits than encoding them separately.

Next we look at the concept of conditional entropy. In the bear example, we want to find the entropy of Y given that we know what quadrant the bear is in. For the four quadrants we have:

$$
\begin{aligned}
H(Y|1) &= -p(H|1)\log p(H|1) - p(L|1)\log p(L|1) \\
&= 0.46899559 \\
H(Y|2) &= -p(H|2)\log p(H|2) - p(L|2)\log p(L|2) \\
&= 0.88129090 \\
H(Y|3) &= -p(H|3)\log p(H|3) - p(L|3)\log p(L|3) \\
&= 0.46899559 \\
H(Y|4) &= -p(H|4)\log p(H|4) - p(L|4)\log p(L|4) \\
&= 0.88129090
\end{aligned}
\tag{42}
$$

This shows that knowing what quadrant the bear is in reduces the entropy of the altitude Y. The entropy is reduced more for quadrants 1 and 3 since there is a much higher difference in the percentages of the two types of terrain than there is for quadrants 2 and 4. Let $H(Y|X)$ be the average conditional entropy of Y given X then

$$
H(Y|X) = \sum_{i=1}^{4} H(Y|i)p(i)
\tag{43}
$$

We can write $H(Y|i)$ as follows

$$
H(Y|i) = - \sum_{j=H,L} p(j|i)\log p(j|i)
\tag{44}
$$

Substituting this into equation 43 gives

$$
\begin{aligned}
H(Y|X) &= -\sum_{i=1}^{4}\sum_{j=H,L} p(j|i)p(i)\log p(j|i)\\
&= -\sum_{i=1}^{4}\sum_{j=H,L} p(i,j)\log p(j|i) \qquad (45)
\end{aligned}
$$

This expression is usually just referred to as the conditional entropy of Y given X. Putting in the numbers for the bear example we get $H(Y|X) = 0.6751432464$. If we substitute $p(j|i) = p(i,j)/p(i)$ into equation 45 then we get the following general result which applies to any two random variables X and Y.

$$
H(Y|X) = H(X,Y) - H(X) \qquad (46)
$$

Likewise it is easy to show that

$$
H(X|Y) = H(X,Y) - H(Y) \qquad (47)
$$

Note that in general, conditional entropy is not symmetric, $H(Y|X)$ is not necessarily equal to $H(X|Y)$. In the bear example we have $H(Y|X) = 0.6751432464$

while $H(X|Y) = 1.704192$. There is more uncertainty in the quadrant given the elevation than there is in the elevation given the quadrant.

Another important quantity related to entropy is called mutual information. This is a measure of the amount of information common to two random variables. If $H(X)$ is the amount of information (uncertainty) contained in X then the conditional entropy $H(X|Y)$ is the amount of information that remains in X after Y is known. The difference $H(X) - H(X|Y)$ is the amount of information about X that is provided by Y. This quantity is called the mutual information of X and Y and is defined as follows.

$$
\begin{aligned}
I(X,Y) &= H(X) - H(X|Y) \\
&= -\sum_i p(i) \log p(i) + \sum_{i,j} p(i,j) \log p(i|j) \\
&= -\sum_{i,j} p(i,j) \log p(i) + \sum_{i,j} p(i,j) \log \frac{p(i,j)}{p(j)} \\
&= \sum_{i,j} p(i,j) \log \frac{p(i,j)}{p(i)p(j)} \qquad (48)
\end{aligned}
$$

Looking at this definition in terms of the joint distribution, $p(i,j)$, and the marginal distributions $p(i)$ and $p(j)$, it is clear that $I(X,Y)$ is also a measure of the dependence of X and Y. If the variables are independent then the joint distribution factors $p(i,j) = p(i)p(j)$ and the mutual information is zero, $I(X,Y) = 0$. One variable provides no information about the other when they are independent.

The definition also shows that mutual information is symmetric, $I(X,Y) = I(Y,X)$, so that X provides as much information about Y as Y provides about X. $I(X,Y)$ can therefore be expressed in the following equivalent ways.

$$\begin{aligned}
I(X,Y) &= H(X) - H(X|Y) \\
&= H(Y) - H(Y|X) \\
&= H(X) + H(Y) - H(X,Y) \quad (49)
\end{aligned}$$

Mutual information will be useful when we look at the concept of channel capacity in a later chapter. If X is the input to a communication channel and Y is the output then, assuming information is lost due to noise in the channel, we want to know how much information about X is provided by Y, i.e. how much information gets through the channel. The mutual information $I(X,Y)$ is a measure of this.

The relationships between joint entropy, conditional entropy, and mutual information of X and Y can be conveniently represented by the Venn diagram shown in figure 17.

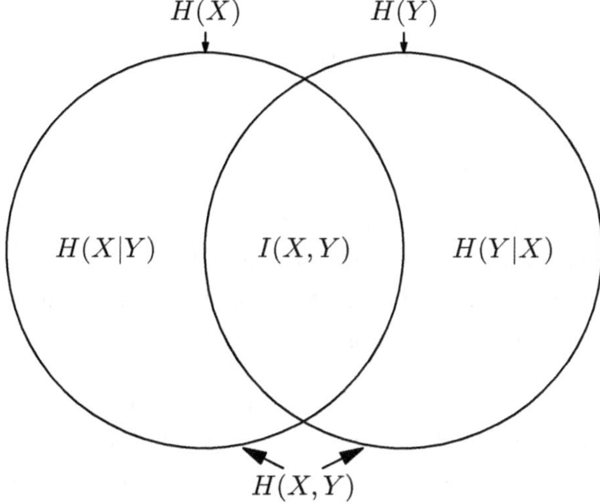

Figure 17: Relationship between joint entropy, conditional entropy, and mutual information.

The two circles represent the information in X and Y and their area of overlap, or intersection, is their mutual information.

Entropy of a Markov Chain

Now we take a short introductory look at calculating the entropy of a source that is described by a model known as a Markov chain. So far we have only considered sources with symbol (message) probabilities that are constant and independent of each other. The series of symbols produced by such a source can be represented as a series of independent and identically distributed random variables.

A more realistic model for many sources is one where the probabilities for the next symbol depend on what the last few symbols were. Language is a good example of such a source. In English for example, the letter u is much more likely than w to follow the letter q.

In general, the dependency can extend back to the last one, two, three, or more symbols. To keep things simple, we will restrict ourselves to sources where the probabilities for the next symbol depend only on the last symbol. Such a source is called a first order Markov chain.

A Markov chain consists of a set of states where each

state has its own set of output probabilities. When a symbol is output, the chain will transition to another state or back to the same state depending on what the output symbol was.

In figure 18 we have an example of a two state Markov chain that emits only the symbols 0 and 1. If the first symbol is 0 then we start in the state labeled 0. From here there is a probability $P(1|0) = a$ that the next symbol is 1 and a probability $P(0|0) = 1 - a$ that the next symbol is 0. If the next symbol is 1 then we transition to the state labeled 1. If the next symbol is 0 then we stay in state 0. In state 1 there is a probability $P(0|1) = b$ that the next symbol is 0 and a probability $P(1|1) = 1 - b$ that the next symbol is 1.

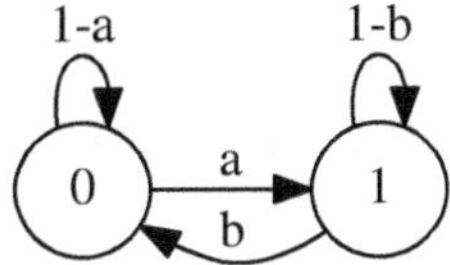

Figure 18: Binary Markov chain.

Each state has its own entropy, which for this simple two state model, is the binary entropy function $H(a) = a \log a + (1 - a) \log (1 - a)$ for state 0 and $H(b) = b \log b + (1 - b) \log (1 - b)$ for state 1. The entropy for the chain is then $H(a)$ times the probability of being in state 0 plus $H(b)$ times the probability of being in state 1. Let μ_0 and μ_1 be the steady state probabilities of being in states 0 and 1 respectively, then they must satisfy the equations

$$\begin{aligned}
\mu_0 &= (1-a)\mu_0 + b\mu_1 \\
\mu_1 &= a\mu_0 + (1-b)\mu_1 \\
\mu_0 + \mu_1 &= 1
\end{aligned} \tag{50}$$

The first equation says that the probability of being in state 0 is equal to the probability, $(1-a)\mu_0$, of being in state 0 and transitioning back to state 0, plus the probability, $b\mu_1$ of being in state 1 and transitioning to state 0. The second equation says likewise for the probability of being in state 1. The third equation says that the chain must be in state 0 or state 1, there are no other alternatives. Solving these equations gives:

$$\mu_0 = \frac{b}{a+b} \tag{51}$$

$$\mu_1 = \frac{a}{a+b} \tag{52}$$

The entropy for the binary Markov chain is then

$$H(a, b) = \frac{b}{a+b} H(a) + \frac{a}{a+b} H(b) \qquad (53)$$

The same basic procedure can be used to work out the entropy for Markov chains with larger numbers of states.

Principle of Maximum Entropy

We end the chapter by looking at a simple example using the principle of maximum entropy. This is a technique for inferring a probability distribution that was first developed by the American physicist Edwin T. Jaynes in a paper titled "Information Theory and Statistical Mechanics" (see references). The general idea is to choose a probability distribution that is consistent with what is known and that does not make any unwarranted assumptions.

Knowledge is expressed as a set of constraint equations that are generally insufficient to uniquely solve for the distribution. The extra condition imposed, is that the correct distribution should be the one that maximizes the entropy. This is the distribution that introduces no additional assumptions. The idea is best understood with a very simple example.

Sparky is a tattoo artist who offers three different tattoos priced at \$8, \$12, and \$16. At the end of the week he knows how many tattoos he did in total and how much money he made but he forgot to keep track of how many of the three different tattoos were sold. He asks Spike, his mathematician friend, to help him figure it out. Taking the total amount Sparky made, A, and dividing by the number of tattoos, N, gives Spike the average cost of a tattoo, $a = A/N$. Letting p_1, p_2, and p_3 be the probabilities of the \$8, \$12, and \$16 tattoos respectively, he can then set up the following equation for the average cost of a tattoo.

$$8p_1 + 12p_2 + 16p_3 = a \tag{54}$$

He gets another equation from the fact that the probabilities must sum to 1.

$$p_1 + p_2 + p_3 = 1 \tag{55}$$

Now Spike has two equations with three unknowns. There are many possible solutions. How can he find the correct one? He decides to use the distribution that maximizes the entropy which is given by

$$H = -p_1 \log(p_1) - p_2 \log(p_2) - p_3 \log(p_3) \tag{56}$$

Using equations 54 and 55 he can write p_2 and p_3 as follows

$$p_2 = 4 - \frac{a}{4} - 2p_1 \tag{57}$$

$$p_3 = \frac{a}{4} - 3 + p_1 \tag{58}$$

Substituting these into equation 56 gives him an expression for the entropy in terms of the probability p_1. Next he finds the maximum of $H(p_1)$ by taking the derivative with respect to p_1, setting the result equal to zero and solving for p_1. Checking to make sure he has a maximum and not a minimum, he gets the following expression for the value of p_1 that maximizes the entropy.

$$p_1(a) = \frac{52 - 3a - \sqrt{64 - 3(a - 12)^2}}{24} \tag{59}$$

The value of a must be in the range $[8, 12]$. At $a = 8$ all the tattoos must have been the \$8 tattoo and at $a = 16$

they must all have been the \$16 tattoo. Checking, he gets $p_1(8) = 1$ and $p_1(16) = 0$ which is correct. A plot of the three probabilities as a function of a is shown in figure 19.

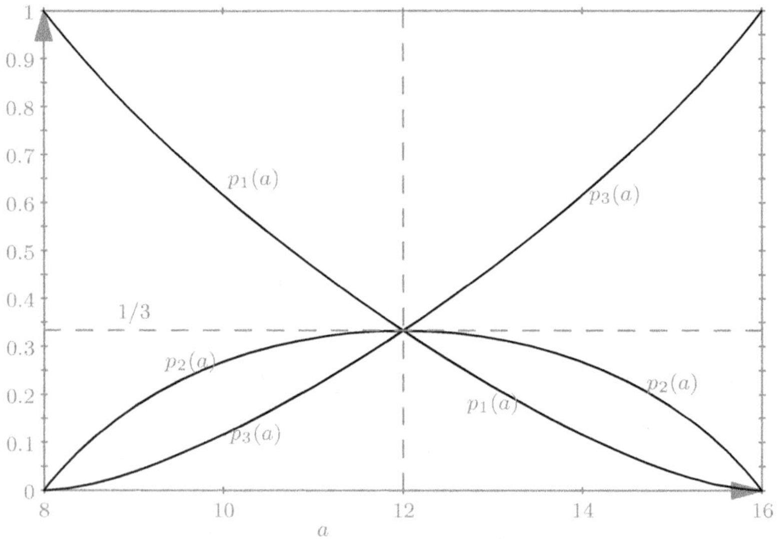

Figure 19: Tattoo probabilities as a function of a.

The constraints $p_1(8) = 1$ and $p_1(16) = 0$ could have been inferred without using the maximum entropy principle so that a reasonable assumption is $p_1(a) = (16 - a)/8$. For $a = 12$, this would result in the probabilities $p_1(12) = 1/2$, $p_2(12) = 0$, and $p_3(12) = 1/2$. The entropy would then be $H = 1$. Using maximum entropy we get $p_1(12) = p_2(12) = p_3(12) = 1/3$ and the entropy is $H = \log(3) = 1.5849625\ldots$ The higher entropy is a result of making fewer assumptions, i.e. no \$12 tattoos were sold.

This time Spike has saved the day, but what happens if Sparky adds some more tattoos to his portfolio? With $N > 3$ tattoos, the problem starts to become more complicated. In what follows, we will work out the problem for general N. The mathematics is somewhat more complicated and can be skipped if desired. The results are not used in the rest of the book.

The general problem is to maximize the entropy

$$H = -\sum_{i=1}^{N} p_i \log p_i \tag{60}$$

subject to the constraints

$$\sum_{i=1}^{N} p_i = 1 \tag{61}$$

$$\sum_{i=1}^{N} p_i x_i = m \tag{62}$$

where the x_i are values of the random variable X and p_i is the probability that $X = x_i$. The mean is m. The givens are m and the x_i values. We want to find the p_i values that maximize H subject to the constraints.

We will do this by using the method of Lagrange multipliers. What this simply means is that we introduce two new variables, α and λ, that will allow us to incorporate the constraints into a new function called the Lagrangian, which is defined as follows

$$L = H + \alpha \left(\sum_{i=1}^{N} p_i - 1 \right) + \lambda \left(\sum_{i=1}^{N} p_i x_i - m \right) \tag{63}$$

The entropy will be maximized when the derivatives of L with respect to α, λ and the p_i's vanish. The derivatives with respect to α and λ are satisfied by the constraints.

$$\frac{\partial L}{\partial \alpha} = \sum_{i=1}^{N} p_i - 1 = 0 \tag{64}$$

$$\frac{\partial L}{\partial \lambda} = \sum_{i=1}^{N} p_i x_i - m = 0 \tag{65}$$

Taking the derivative with respect to p_i we have

$$\frac{\partial L}{\partial p_i} = \frac{\partial H}{\partial p_i} + \alpha + \lambda x_i = 0 \tag{66}$$

$$\frac{\partial H}{\partial p_i} = -\log p_i - 1 \tag{67}$$

Solving these last two equations for $\log p_i$ we get $\log p_i = \alpha - 1 + \lambda x_i$ so that $p_i = e^{\alpha-1}e^{\lambda x_i}$. To satisfy the first constraint, we must have $e^{\alpha-1} = \left(\sum_{i=1}^{N} e^{\lambda x_i}\right)^{-1}$. This gives us the following expression for p_i

$$p_i = \frac{e^{\lambda x_i}}{\sum_{i=1}^{N} e^{\lambda x_i}} \tag{68}$$

It remains to determine λ. This can be done by substituting the expression we just found for p_i into the second constraint equation. This gives us

$$\sum_{i=1}^{N} x_i e^{\lambda x_i} = m \sum_{i=1}^{N} e^{\lambda x_i} \tag{69}$$

This equation can be solved for λ. One way to do it is to define $y = e^{\lambda}$ and then rewrite the equation as

$$\sum_{i=1}^{N} (x_i - m)y^{x_i} = 0 \tag{70}$$

Find the smallest positive real root of this equation and use that as the value for y. The p_i values can then also be calculated directly in terms of y as

$$p_i = \frac{y^{x_i}}{\sum_{i=1}^{N} y^{x_i}} \tag{71}$$

One unstated assumption that we made in deriving these equations is that the mean m is greater than the smallest x_i value and less than the largest x_i value. If they are ordered so that $x_1 < x_2 < \cdots < x_N$ then we must have $x_1 < m < x_N$. If $m = x_1$ then $p_1 = 1$ and all other p_i are zero. If $m = x_N$ then $p_N = 1$ and all other p_i are zero. For all other values of m within the range, the p_i values can be calculated using equation 71.

ENTROPY OF ENGLISH

Calculating the entropy of the English language is an excellent example of the use of higher order statistical models. Claude Shannon used it as an example in the first paper ever published on information theory. He also looked at the subject in greater detail in a second paper solely devoted to it (see references). When he looked at the problem of calculating the entropy of English there were fewer statistics available than there are today. With modern computer technology it is possible to collect statistics from millions of English texts. In this chapter we will use these statistics to update some of Shannon's calculations.

English text is a source where there are strong statistical dependencies between the symbols being produced. For example the letter h often follows the letter t but this strongly depends on what comes before the t. Another rule is that u almost always follows q. These dependencies reduce the information content (entropy) of English text.

When you randomly delete some of the letters in a text, a good native speaker can often reconstruct it. Clearly the deleted letters represent redundant information. Shannon showed that by using a process where native speakers guess the series of letters in a text, he could get a good estimate for the entropy of English. The idea is that a native speaker has an intimate knowledge of the structure of the language and can use long range dependencies to guess the next letter. The speaker is essentially being used as a source of statistical knowledge about the language.

Instead of using a native speaker, we will estimate the entropy by using statistics on what are called n-grams. An n-gram is simply a string of n letters found in ordinary English text. We use the term ordinary in the sense that these are not specialized texts, containing jargon and abbreviations that are not common knowledge.

The sequence of letters in a text are not independent. This means the amount of information provided by each new letter depends on the letters that came before it. Another way of saying this is that the uncertainty of the next letter depends on the preceeding letters. If a word begins with a q then it is fairly certain the next letter will be a u.

The dependencies are taken into account in the calculation of the conditional entropy $F_n = H(Y|X_n)$, where X_n is a series of n letters, i.e. an n-gram, and Y is the next letter in the series. Increasing n will take into account longer range dependencies. The entropy is then equal to the limit as n becomes very large:

$$H = \lim_{n \to \infty} F_n \tag{72}$$

For some languages it may be true that no statistical dependencies extend beyond a finite number of symbols, m, in which case $H = F_m$. As a practical matter, calculating F_m for large m may be impossible if the number of symbols is large. For English, excluding punctuation, we have 26 letters and the space, so there are $27^5 = 14,348,907$ 5-grams. For large n there are simply too many n-grams for reliable statistics.

The conditional entropy F_n is calculated as follows:

$$\begin{aligned}
F_n &= -\sum_{Y,X_n} p(Y, X_n) \log p(Y|X_n) \\
&= -\sum_{Y,X_n} p(Y, X_n) \log p(Y, X_n) + \\
&\quad \sum_{Y,X_n} p(Y, X_n) \log p(X_n) \\
&= H(Y, X_n) - H(X_n)
\end{aligned} \tag{73}$$

The term $H(X_n)$ is the entropy for the set of n-grams while $H(Y, X_n)$ is the entropy for the set of (n+1)-grams.

We will calculate three increasingly accurate entropy approximations of English, which we'll call zero, first and second order.

For zero order entropy, the crudest approximation, all letters are equally probable so the probability of any one letter is 1/26. Equation 31 then gives
$H_0 = \log_2(26) = 4.70044$.

For first order entropy, we use the probability of letters in an English text. In other words, if we were to randomly select a letter in an English text, what is the probability that it is an "a", a "b", and so on. The statistical model is that the letters are independent. The probability of the next letter is not a function of the current letter. We can find these probabilities by looking at single letter, or 1-gram counts, as given by Norvig.[5] They are converted to probabilities, and shown in table 2.

Using the 1-gram probabilities in table 2, we can calculate the entropy using equation 31. This gives us $H_1 = 4.16541$ which has been reduced from the zero order approximation of 4.7.

For 2nd order entropy, we use bigram (2-gram) probabilities. These are probabilities of letter pairs. The assumption here is that the probability of the next letter in an English text depends only on the current letter.

---

[5]http://norvig.com/mayzner.html

1-gram	count	probability
E	445155370175	0.124921
T	330535289102	0.0927556
A	286527429118	0.0804061
O	272276534337	0.0764069
I	269731642485	0.0756928
N	257770795264	0.0723363
S	232082812755	0.0651277
R	223767519675	0.0627942
H	180074687596	0.050533
L	144998552911	0.0406899
D	136017528785	0.0381696
C	119155568598	0.0334377
U	97273082907	0.027297
M	89506734085	0.0251176
F	85635440629	0.0240312
P	76112599849	0.0213589
G	66615316232	0.0186938
W	59712390260	0.0167566
Y	59331661972	0.0166498
B	52905544693	0.0148465
V	37532682260	0.0105325
K	19261229433	0.00540513
X	8369138754	0.00234857
J	5657910830	0.00158774
Q	4292916949	0.00120469
Z	3205398166	0.000899507

Table 2: 1-gram counts and probabilities.

We get the bigram probabilities by combining Norvig's bigram counts with bigram space counts (a single letter preceeded or followed by a space). That data is gotten from columns */1:1 and */-1:-1 in Norvig's 1-gram counts. The total number of bigrams, including spaces, is over 700, some of which are shown in table 3 with their probabilities (spaces are indicated by a dash).

The bigram probabilities of table 2 gives an entropy of 7.49069. To get the second order entropy, we must use equation 73, subtracting that of the 1-grams, giving $H_2 = 7.49069 - 4.16541 = 3.32528$.
In comparison, Shannon calculated in his paper "Prediction and Entropy of Printed English" (pg 51) a value of $7.70 - 4.14 = 3.56$ bits/letter.

At this point we could go on using 3-grams and higher to get increasingly accurate estimates of the entropy. Instead we will look at estimating the entropy using words instead of letters. We can get the frequencies of words in the English language from Norvig's common words count file. The first 25 most common words are shown in table 4. Using a total of $97,565$ words and their probabilities, we calculate the first order word entropy to be 10.6803.

To convert the word entropy into entropy per character, we need to divide by the average length of a word. A histogram of word lengths is shown in figure 20. The shortest word has length one and the

Bigram	count	probability
TH	100272945963	0.0232795
HE	86697336727	0.0201278
IN	68595215308	0.0159252
ER	57754162106	0.0134083
AN	55974567611	0.0129951
RE	52285662239	0.0121387
ON	49570981965	0.0115085
AT	41920838452	0.0097324
EN	41004903554	0.00951975
ND	38129777631	0.00885226
TI	37856196209	0.00878875
ES	37766388079	0.0087679
OR	35994097756	0.00835644
TE	33973261529	0.00788728
...	...	...
-V	6129410533	0.00142301
V-	407828700	9.46821e-05
-K	3390029632	0.000787034
K-	5966068064	0.00138509
-X	335403585	7.78678e-05
X-	1228057066	0.000285107
-J	3801073430	0.000882462
J-	161332557	3.74552e-05
-Q	1647734497	0.00038254
Q-	93340457	2.167e-05
-Z	336016172	7.801e-05
Z-	241774733	5.61308e-05

Table 3: Bigram counts and probabilities.

word	count	probability
THE	53097401461	0.0713825
OF	30966074232	0.0416299
AND	22632024504	0.0304258
TO	19347398077	0.0260101
IN	16891065263	0.0227078
A	15310087895	0.0205824
IS	8384246685	0.0112715
THAT	8000768228	0.010756
FOR	6545282031	0.00879928
IT	5740085369	0.0077168
AS	5700645258	0.00766378
WAS	5502713968	0.00739768
WITH	5182797249	0.0069676
BE	4818864785	0.00647834
BY	4703106084	0.00632271
ON	4594521081	0.00617674
NOT	4522732626	0.00608023
HE	4110457083	0.00552597
I	3884828634	0.00522265
THIS	3826060334	0.00514364
ARE	3700433333	0.00497475
OR	3667713965	0.00493076
HIS	3611377789	0.00485503
FROM	3469207674	0.0046639
AT	3413452256	0.00458894

Table 4: Top 25 word counts and probabilities.

longest word has length 23. The median length of a word is 7.59624 and the average length is 4.79067. Using the average length, we get an entropy per character of $H = 10.6803/4.79067 = 2.23$. This is considerably smaller than the second order entropy, $H_2 = 3.32528$, that we calculated above based on letter bigrams. Since the average word length is 4.79067, we can assume that the word entropy takes into account statistical correlations of at least that length between letters. In other words, to get the same accuracy with letter n-grams we would probably have to use at least 5-grams.

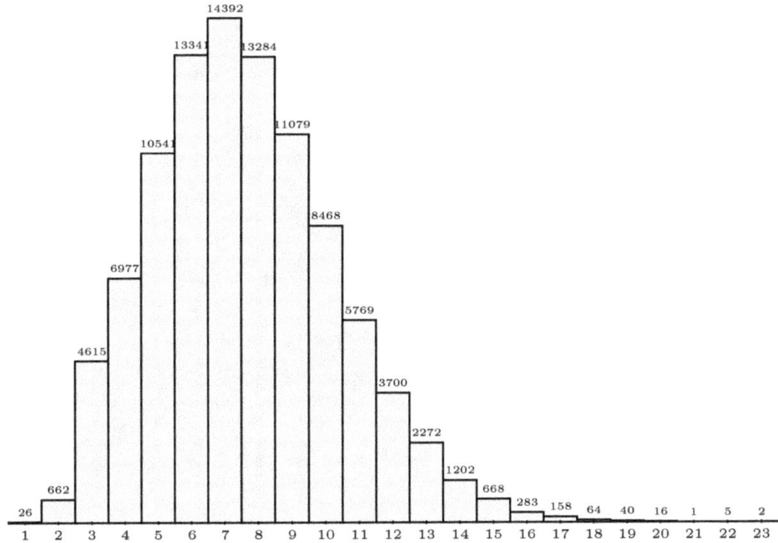

Figure 20: Word length histogram of top $97,565$ most common English words.

Without taking any statistics into account, i.e. assuming all letters are equally probable, we would need a minimum of $\log(27) = 4.755$ bits per character to encode English. The entropy calculation based on single word counts shows that this could in principle be reduced to 2.23 bits per character. This is a more than 50% reduction, showing that the structure of the English language is at least 50% redundant. It should be possible to randomly delete about half the letters in an English text and have a good native speaker reconstruct the text. From the popularity of crossword puzzles and the TV game show "Wheel of Fortune", it seems that guessing missing letters and words is a fun way for people to test their knowledge of English.

CHANNEL CAPACITY

When information is transmitted from source to receiver, the physical medium over which the transmission takes place, called the channel, will often introduce noise into the received signal. The noise may cause the received message to differ from the transmitted message. This also happens when information is stored and then later retrieved. The retrieved information may differ from what was stored, due to noise and imperfections in the storage medium, which plays the role of the channel.

How much information can be transferred over a channel? That is the question we will look at in this chapter. For every channel with noise, there is an upper limit on the rate at which information can be transmitted from source to receiver with an arbitrarily small possibility of error. That rate is called the channel capacity.

Trying to transmit information at a rate greater than the channel capacity will result in errors no matter how cleverly the information is encoded. If the transmission rate is kept below the channel capacity then it is possible to encode the information in such a way as to make the probability of error arbitrarily small. The discovery of this fact is one of the great achievements of information theory. It is known as the noisy channel coding theorem and it was first stated by Shannon in his 1948 paper.

In this chapter we are only going to look at how the channel capacity is calculated. In the next chapter we will look at the topic of how to encode information to reduce the probability of error. That is a large subject in its own right and can be studied independently of the results in this chapter.

To calculate the channel capacity we need a way to characterize the channel. Let X be the random variable representing the input to the channel. This is the message the source wants to send to the receiver. Let Y represent what the receiver actually receives. We will assume that X and Y are both discrete random variables i.e. they can only have one of a finite set of values. Without loss of generality we take those values to be $i = 1, 2, \ldots, N$ for X and $j = 1, 2, \ldots, M$ for Y.

We can completely describe the channel with the conditional probabilities $p(Y = j | X = i)$ which we will write simply as $p(j|i)$. This is the probability that when the source sends the symbol i, the receiver gets the symbol j. With the conditional probabilities and the source probabilities $p(i)$ we can calculate the mutual information $I(X, Y)$, which, as you may recall from the entropy chapter, is a measure of the amount of information common to both X and Y.

$H(X)$ is the amount of information in X and the conditional entropy, $H(X|Y)$, is the amount of information that remains in X after Y is known. Subtracting the two, we get the mutual information, $I(X,Y) = H(X) - H(X|Y)$ which is the amount of information about X that is provided by Y. It is the amount of information that gets through the channel to the receiver. The channel capacity, C, is defined as $I(X,Y)$ maximized over all possible source probability distributions, $p(i)$.

$$C = \max_{p(i)} I(X,Y) \tag{74}$$

Ideally, the channel is noiseless so that $Y = X$ and $H(X|Y) = 0$. The mutual information is then $I(X,Y) = H(X)$. The source entropy, $H(X)$, is maximized when all symbols have the same probability $p(i) = 1/N$, making $H(X) = \log N$. The channel capacity is then $C = \log N$. The channel capacity is difficult to calculate in general but it can be worked out for some simple cases.

The most important simple case is the binary symmetric channel shown in figure 21. The inputs and outputs are 0 or 1. There is an error probability e that the output becomes the complement of the input, i.e. a 0 becomes a 1, or a 1 becomes a 0. The conditional probabilities describing the channel are $p(0|0) = p(1|1) = 1 - e$ and $p(0|1) = p(1|0) = e$. The conditional entropy is $H(X|Y) = H(e)$ where $H(e) = -e \log e - (1 -$

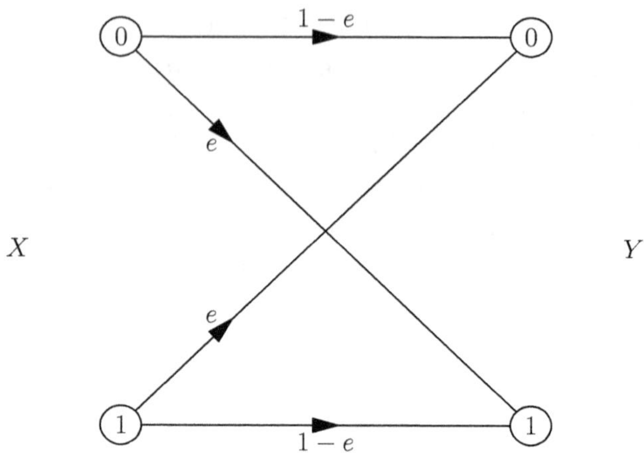

Figure 21: Binary symmetric channel.

$e) \log{(1 - e)}$ is the binary entropy function. The mutual information is $I(X, Y) = H(X) - H(e)$. This is maximized when both inputs have probability $1/2$ so that $H(X) = 1$. The channel capacity for the binary symmetric channel is then

$$C = 1 - H(e) \tag{75}$$

Note that when $e = 1/2$ we have $H(e) = 1$ and the channel capacity becomes zero. In this case, there is no relationship between X and Y. The output of the channel is completely random, so no information can be transmitted. When $e = 0$ we have $H(e) = 0$ and the channel capacity is $C = 1$. With no probability of error, no information is lost and every bit going into the channel arrives at the receiver unchanged.

If the error probability is $e = 1/8$ or 12.5% then $H(1/8) = 0.54356$ and the channel capacity is $C = 1 - H(1/8) = 0.45644$. To send information at below this rate, so as to keep errors to a minimum, the data needs to be encoded. What this means practically, is that every k data bits from the source must be encoded in $n > k$ bits so that the data rate k/n is less than the channel capacity. By increasing k and n so that the ratio k/n approaches the channel capacity from below, it is possible to make the error probability as small as desired. Some ways to do the encoding are discussed in the next chapter.

Channel Capacity and Gambling

The primary significance of the channel capacity comes from its use in Shannon's noisy channel coding theorem. Another somewhat surprising use for the concept of channel capacity is in finding optimal money management schemes for gambling and investments. This was first discovered by the American physicist John Larry Kelly, Jr. who was a colleague of Shannon's at Bell Labs in the 1950s. In 1956 he published a paper titled "A New Interpretation of Information Rate" where he uses a binary channel as a model for betting on the outcome of a series of baseball games.

Suppose for example, that you had a channel which gave you the results of a game before it was played. You could use the information to bet on the game and make money. If the channel was noiseless then you would of course bet all your money on each game and, given even odds, double your money every time. But what if the channel is not noiseless so that the results are occasionally wrong? Betting all your money on each game is then not a good idea since you could loose it all. Kelly showed that by betting a certain fraction of your money on each game you could make it grow at an exponential rate equal to the channel capacity.

Before showing how the betting fraction and the exponential growth rate are related to the channel capacity, we should mention that this situation is not as far fetched as it sounds. What is really being modeled here is a situation where you have information that allows you to predict the outcome of a chance event (like a baseball game) with better than even odds. Let's say you've found a way to analyze the game that lets you predict the outcome correctly 60% of the time. This is equivalent to receiving information about the outcome over a binary channel that has an error probability of $e = 0.4$.

Let a_n represent the amount of money you have after n bets with a_0 being the amount of money you start with. The bets are even money, meaning you get back double what you bet if you win and nothing if you lose. If you can predict the outcome with 100% accuracy then you should put all your money on each bet. After the first bet, you will have $a_1 = 2a_0$, after the second, $a_2 = 2a_1 = 2^2 a_0$ and so on. After n bets, you will have $a_n = 2^n a_0$.

In reality, nothing is predictable with 100% accuracy so there's always a chance you can lose, and you don't want to put all your money on each bet. Instead, let's say you put a fraction f of your money on each bet. If you win the nth bet you will have $a_n = (1+f)a_{n-1}$ and if you lose you will have $a_n = (1-f)a_{n-1}$. If p is the probability that your prediction is correct and $1-p$ is the probability that it is wrong, then we can write the outcome as

$$a_n = (1 + x_n f)a_{n-1} \tag{76}$$

where x_n is a random variable equal to 1 with probability p and -1 with probability $1-p$. Equation 76 can be iterated to give a_n in terms of the initial bankroll a_0 as

$$a_n = a_0 \prod_{i=1}^{n} (1 + x_i f) \tag{77}$$

The initial bankroll is just an overall scale factor so we will assume $a_0 = 1$ in what follows.

Assuming each bet is independent of all the others, we can write the average value (expectation) of the bankroll after n bets as:

$$E[a_n] = \prod_{i=1}^{n} E[1 + x_i f] \tag{78}$$

Using the fact that the expectation for the random variable x_i is $E[x_i] = p - (1 - p) = 2p - 1$, the expectation for the terms in the product is

$$E[1 + x_i f] = 1 + E[x_i]f = 1 + (2p - 1)f \tag{79}$$

and equation 78 then simplifies to

$$E[a_n] = (1 + (2p - 1)f)^n \tag{80}$$

For $p > 1/2$ and $0 < f \leq 1$ this is an increasing function of n that is maximized for $f = 1$. But using $f = 1$ is a problem because one loss will bankrupt you. Trying to maximize the average of a_n is no good.

Let's see what happens if we maximize $\log a_n$ instead. From equation 77 (remember we are using $a_0 = 1$) we have

$$\log a_n = \sum_{i=1}^{n} \log(1 + x_i f) \tag{81}$$

Taking the expectation, we have:

$$E[\log a_n] = \sum_{i=1}^{n} E[\log(1 + x_i f)] \tag{82}$$

The expectation of the terms in the sum is $E[\log(1 + x_i f)] = p \log(1 + f) + (1 - p) \log(1 - f)$ so the equation simplifies to

$$E[\log a_n] = n[p \log(1 + f) + (1 - p) \log(1 - f)] \tag{83}$$

To find the value of f that maximizes this, take the derivative with respect to f, set it equal to zero and solve for f. Verifying that the result is a maximum by making sure the second derivative is negative we get:

$$f = 2p - 1 \tag{84}$$

When $p = 1/2$, which means the prediction is no better than a fair coin toss, we get $f = 0$ which makes sense. If you really can't predict anything then don't bet anything. When $p = 1$, which means the prediction is 100% accurate, we get $f = 1$. If you are certain of the outcome then bet everything. If $p = 3/4$, meaning you can predict accurately 3 out of 4 times, then $f = 1/2$ and you should bet half your money on every game.

Substitute equation 84 into equation 83 and you get

$$
\begin{aligned}
E[\log a_n] &= n[1 + p \log p + (1-p)\log(1-p)] \\
&= n[1 - H(p)] \\
&= nC
\end{aligned}
\tag{85}
$$

where C is the channel capacity for a binary symmetric channel as given in equation 75. This equation says that if you use fixed fraction betting, with the fraction given by equation 84, then, on average, your money will grow exponentially at a rate equal to the channel capacity.

The above analysis can be extended to situations with uneven odds and to situations with more than two results. Investing in a stock is an example of the latter. Over any period you can have many different possible gains and losses on a stock.

There is some evidence that Shannon may have used fixed fraction betting in the stock market but he seems to have mainly invested in companies that he knew well and that he thought would be successful. He did try gambling with this betting system in Las Vegas. For more information on his adventures in gambling, see the book "Fortune's Formula". For more mathematical background on fixed fraction betting and investing, see "Bet Smart: The Kelly System for Gambling and Investing".

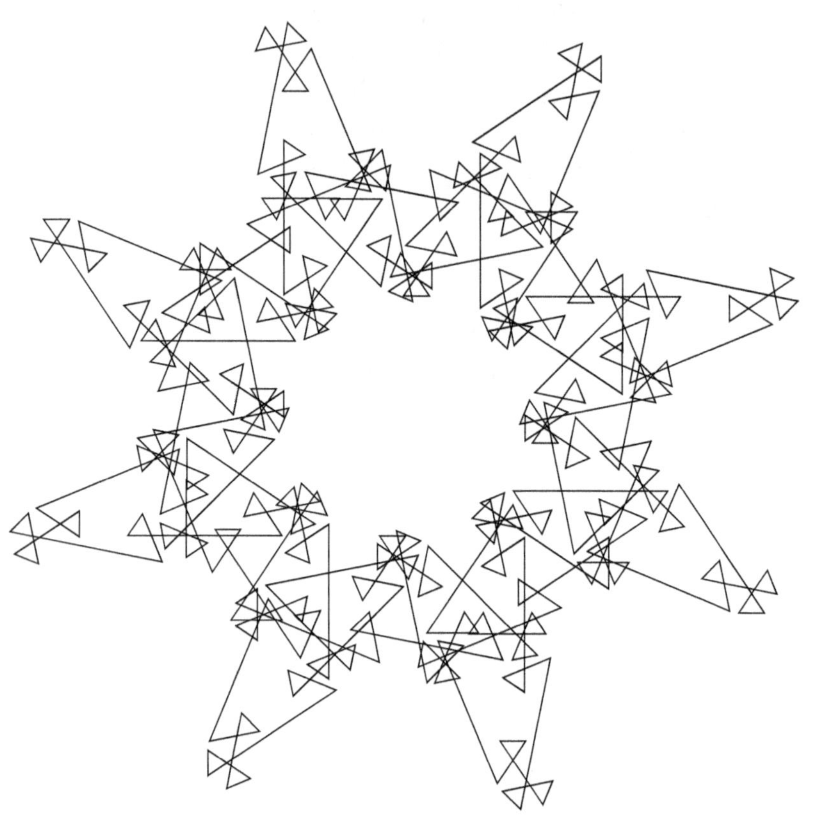

ERROR CORRECTION CODING

In previous chapters we looked at how to encode messages as efficiently as possible, i.e. using the least number of bits. This is known as source coding or data compression. Now we want to look at another major topic related to information theory called error correction or channel coding.

When information is transmitted over space or time it may accumulate errors due to noise in the transmission channel. With error correction coding we want to represent information in a way that allows errors to be corrected or at least detected. This involves adding some redundancy which makes it the opposite of source coding where redundancy is removed. A good communication system will use both source and channel coding. Source coding almost always comes first followed by channel coding.

Error correction coding is a vast subject that can be studied almost independently of the rest of information theory. An entire book could easily be devoted to it alone. Indeed many books on the subject have been written (see references). In this chapter we will only scratch the surface of the subject by looking at a few simple coding techniques.

All the codes we will look at can be classified as (n, k) binary codes. This notation signifies that each code word is an n bit binary number and that k of those bits are message or data bits. Obviously we must have $n \geq k$. The remaining $n - k$ bits are code bits used to detect and/or correct any errors in the message bits. The k message bits are often placed in a block at the beginning of the code word but they may also be interspersed with the code bits.

A useful way to visualize the error coding process is to think of the k message bits as being k dimensional binary vectors (all k vector components are 0 or 1). There are 2^k such vectors. These vectors are mapped to an n dimensional code space. In code space there are 2^n possible binary vectors of which only 2^k are code vectors that represent legitimate code words. The remaining $2^n - 2^k$ vectors are error vectors where there is an error in either the message or code bits.

An intuitive picture of what happens in error correction coding is shown in figure 22. The figure illustrates message vectors being mapped to code vectors in a higher dimensional code space. The channel coder at the transmitter does the mapping and transmits the code vector. If no error occurs then the receiver can decode the code vector (map it back to message space) and retrieve the message.

If only a small number of errors occur then the receiver will get a vector that is in the neighborhood of one of the code vectors. These neighborhoods are represented by the circles in figure 22. The receiver finds the code vector that is closest to the vector it received and assumes that it is the correct code vector.

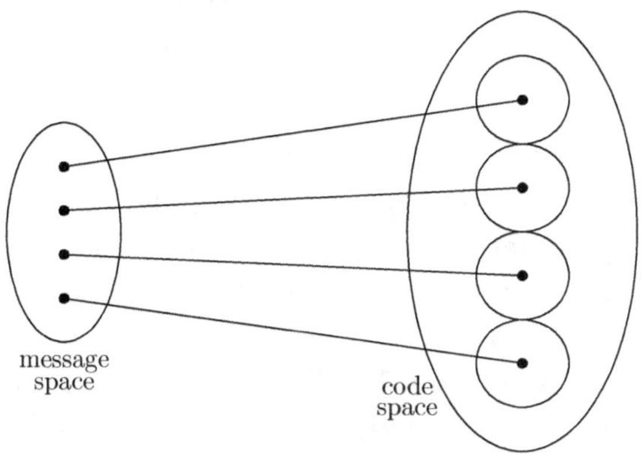

Figure 22: Message to code space mapping.

This process can obviously not correct all errors. If too many errors occur it may put the received vector in the neighborhood of the wrong code vector or it may turn the received vector into a code vector different from the one transmitted. The basic trick is to make the neighborhood of each code vector large enough so that the probability of a decoding mistake is very small. Next we will look at some simple examples of error correction coding.

Repetition Codes

Probably the simplest example is the single bit repetition code. This is an $(n, 1)$ code where each data bit is repeated n times. For binary data there are only two code words consisting of either all 0's or all 1's. For example with $n = 3$, the two code words are 000 and 111.

The receiver uses a simple majority rule to decide which data bit was actually sent. The words 000, 001, 010, 100 are all decoded as 0. For the last three, the assumption is that one error occurred during transmission, changing a 0 to a 1. Likewise, the words 111, 110, 101, 011 are all decoded as 1. This coding scheme can correct for single errors. With more than one error the receiver will make a decoding mistake.

What is the probability of a decoding mistake with this code? Assume the error probabilities for the three bits are independent and equal to p. There will be a decoding mistake when 2 or 3 errors occur. The probability of two and three errors are $3p^2(1 - p)$ and p^3 respectively. The probability of a decoding mistake is then $3p^2(1 - p) + p^3 = (3 - 2p)p^2$. With $p = 0.1$ the probability is 0.028. The $(3, 1)$ repetition code has reduced the probability from 10% to just under 3%.

In general, for the $(n, 1)$ repetition code, n should be odd to avoid a situation where the receiver gets a word with the same number of 0's and 1's. Such a word cannot be decoded. When n is odd, the code can correct up to $(n-1)/2$ errors. With $(n+1)/2$ or more errors there will be a decoding mistake.

Question: For odd n, find the probability of a decoding error using the $(n, 1)$ repetition code. Assume that bit errors are independent with probability equal to p.

Answer: A decoding error will occur when a majority of the bits are in error. When n is odd, a majority of the bits is $(n+1)/2$ or more bits. The number of ways that k out of n bits can be in error is the number of ways of choosing k out of n bits without regard for order. That number is given by the binomial coefficient $\binom{n}{k}$. Each of these ways has probability equal to $p^k(1-p)^{n-k}$. Summing over all possible values for k gives the following probability of a decoding error.

$$\sum_{k=\frac{n+1}{2}}^{n} \binom{n}{k} p^k (1-p)^{n-k} \tag{86}$$

The problem with a repetition code is that it is very inefficient. Every bit must be transmitted n times. The data rate (ratio of data bits to total bits) for this code is $1/n$ which goes to zero for large n. This means there is no way this code can approach the channel capacity (see previous chapter).

Parity Check Codes

If it is possible to signal for re-transmission of the data, then we could just try to detect an error instead of correct it. One way to do that is with a simple parity check.

An even parity check code will add an extra bit, called the parity bit, to the end of the data bits so that the total number of 1's is always even. For example if the data bits are 1100 then there are already an even number of 1's so a 0 is added to the end to produce the code word 11000. For data bits 0100 there are an odd number of 1's so a 1 is added to the end to produce the code word 01001.

The receiver checks for a transmission error by summing the bits and dividing by 2. If the remainder is not 0, i.e. the sum is not even, then an error has occurred. This is called a parity check. The method can detect any odd number of errors. An even number of errors will go undetected.

The parity check idea can also be used for error correction. We can, for example, take four consecutive blocks of four data bits and arrange them in a square array as follows

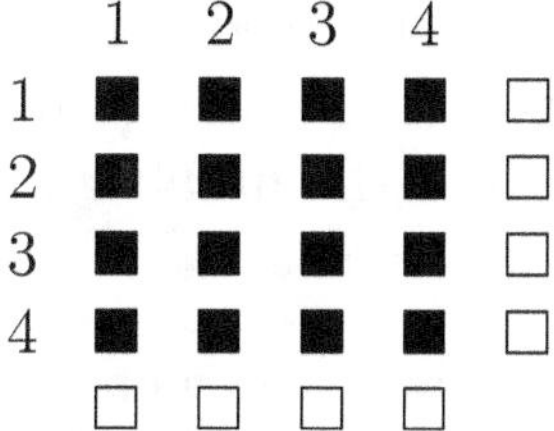

where the black squares represent data bits and the white squares represent parity check bits. The bits at the end of each row are parity checks for the data bits in that row. The bits at the bottom of each column are parity checks for the data bits in that column. The receiver does a parity check of each row and column. It is clear that if one of the data bits is in error then the parity checks for the row and column of that bit will fail and the data bit can be identified and corrected. For example if the parity check for row 2 and column 3 fail then we can assume that the data bit at row 2 and column 3 is in error. The method is not fool proof since the parity bits themselves may be in error.

Hamming Codes

This idea of running redundant parity checks over the data bits is the basic idea behind what is called a Hamming code. Like in the square array, the parity bits in a Hamming code are used to check different, but possibly overlapping, subsets of the data bits. The subsets are chosen so that the parity checks can be used to construct a number called the syndrome. If the syndrome is 0 it indicates no error otherwise it is the number of the bit that is in error.

With m parity checks it is possible to construct 2^m syndrome numbers since each check has two possible outcomes, pass or fail, 0 or 1. So the m parity checks can produce the 2^m numbers $0, 1, 2, \ldots, 2^m - 1$. The number 0 indicates no error and the rest of the numbers indicate the number of the bit that is in error. This means that with k data bits, m parity bits, and the no error condition, we must have $2^m \geq m + k + 1$.

We will illustrate how all this works with an example. Using $m = 3$ parity checks we can correct $k = 2^m - m - 1 = 4$ data bits. The code word is 7 bits long with 4 data bits, d_1, d_2, d_3, d_4 and 3 parity check bits, c_1, c_2, c_3. In the code word, the parity check bits are placed at positions 1, 2, and 4 and the rest of the bits are data bits so the code word looks like the following

Code word: c_1 c_2 d_1 c_3 d_2 d_3 d_4
Bit number: 1   2   3   4   5   6   7

The parity bit c_1 is used to parity check bits $1, 3, 5, 7$, c_2 is used to check bits $2, 3, 6, 7$ and c_3 is used to check bits $4, 5, 6, 7$. When the receiver gets the code word, it constructs the three bit syndrome $s_3 s_2 s_1$. s_1 is set to the parity of bits covered by c_1 i.e. if the sum of bits $1, 3, 5, 7$ is even, then $s_1 = 0$, otherwise $s_1 = 1$. s_2 is set to the parity of the bits covered by c_2 (bits $2, 3, 6, 7$). s_3 is set to the parity of the bits covered by c_3 (bits $4, 5, 6, 7$). The syndrome gives the error number. A 0 means no error, any other number is the number of the bit in error.

Suppose now that there is an error in the second data bit, d_2, which is bit number 5 in the code word. Parity check bits c_1 and c_3 both cover bit number 5, so those parity checks will fail and syndrome bits s_1 and s_3 will equal 1. The syndrome number is then $s_3 s_2 s_1 = 101 = 5$ which is the bit number of d_2 in the code word.

The Hamming $(7, 4)$ code is a fairly efficient code, providing a data rate of $4/7 = 0.5714$. It is possible to construct larger Hamming codes that encode larger numbers of data bits in each code word. In a Hamming code, m parity bits can encode $k = 2^m - m - 1$ data bits. The total number of bits in a code word is $n = k + m = 2^m - 1$ so the data rate for a Hamming code is $k/n = 1 - m/(2^m - 1)$. Hamming codes have the highest possible data rate for their size and distance between code words. They are part of a large class of codes called linear codes and both the encoding and decoding operations can be represented in terms of matrices.

There are many other types of codes besides what we have covered here, such as BCH, Golay, Reed-Solomon, and Reed-Muller codes but this is as far as we will go into the subject of error correction coding. As we said at the beginning, error correction coding is a very large subject in its own right and what we have covered is only a bare minimal introduction. We encourage the reader to explore this fascinating subject in greater depth. In the references you will find more books on the subject.

Supplementary Material

REVIEW OF LOGARITHMS

Taking the logarithm of y in base b is equivalent to solving the equation $y = b^x$ for the number x. In other words we want to find the number x such that b raised to the power of x is equal to y. The logarithm of y in base b is written as $x = \log_b(y)$. For example, the base 2 logarithm of 8 is 3 since $8 = 2^3$. The base 2 logarithm of 16 is 4 since $16 = 2^4$.

One of the most useful properties of logarithms is that they can turn multiplication and division into addition and subtraction, respectively. The logarithm of the product $y_1 y_2$ is the sum of their logarithms. In any arbitrary base we have

$$\log(y_1 y_2) = \log(y_1) + \log(y_2)$$

To see this, just write $y_1 = b^{x_1}$ and $y_2 = b^{x_2}$ so that by definition $x_1 = \log(y_1)$ and $x_2 = \log(y_2)$. The product is then $y_1 y_2 = b^{x_1} b^{x_2} = b^{x_1 + x_2}$ so that by definition $x_1 + x_2 = \log(y_1 y_2)$. Likewise, it is easy to show that for division we have

$$\log\left(\frac{y_1}{y_2}\right) = \log(y_1) - \log(y_2)$$

A corollary of the rule that multiplication becomes addition is the rule that the logarithm of a number raised to a power is the logarithm of that number times the power

$$\log(y^r) = r\log(y)$$

From this it is easy to derive the formula for converting a logarithm in base b to a logarithm in base a. If x is the base a logarithm of y then $y = a^x$. Take the base b logarithm of both sides of this equation and you get $\log_b(y) = x\log_b(a)$ solving for x we get

$$x = \frac{\log_b(y)}{\log_b(a)}$$

That covers most of the basic properties of logarithms that we will find useful. One more identity that will be useful in the chapter on channel capacity is for the derivative of a logarithm

$$\frac{d}{dy}\log_b(y) = \frac{1}{y\ln(b)}$$

where the function $\ln(b)$ signifies the natural logarithm of b. This is the logarithm to the base $e = 2.718281828459\ldots$. One of the ways to define the number e is as the limit

$$e = \lim_{n \to \infty} \left(1 + \frac{1}{n}\right)$$

If x is the logarithm of y in any arbitrary base b then it can can be expressed in terms of the natural logarithm as follows

$$x = \frac{\ln(y)}{\ln(b)}$$

This means that only a method for calculating natural logarithms is needed. One way to calculate the natural logarithm is with the following infinite series which converges quickly when y is not too large.

$$\ln(y) = 2 \sum_{k=0}^{\infty} \frac{1}{2k+1} \left(\frac{y-1}{y+1}\right)^{2k+1}$$

Functions for taking the natural logarithm and logarithms to any base can be found in most mathematical software packages and on most calculators, so there is often no need to implement this calculation. Functions for finding a rational approximation to a logarithm in any base are sometimes useful and rarely found in most software packages. We present a basic algorithm for finding rational approximations of logarithms that is based on Shank's algorithm (see references). To find the base b logarithm of a, we want to find the number x such that $a = b^x$. Start by finding the integer n_1 such that $b^{n_1} < a < b^{n_1+1}$. x will then be contained in the interval $(n_1, n_1 + 1)$ and there is a number $1/x_1 < 1$ such that $x = n_1 + 1/x_1$ and $a = b^{n_1+1/x_1}$. Define a new variable b_2 and set it equal to the result of dividing both sides of the last equation by b^{n_1}, so we have

$$b_2 = \frac{a}{b^{n_1}} = b^{1/x_1}$$

which we can write as $b = b_2^{x_1}$. Solving this for x_1 is equivalent to solving our original equation, $a = b^x$, for x so we can follow the same procedure as above to get an integer n_2 such that $x_1 = n_2 + 1/x_2$. We now have

$$\begin{aligned} x &= n_1 + \frac{1}{x_1} \\[2em] &= n_1 + \cfrac{1}{n_2 + \cfrac{1}{x_2}} \end{aligned}$$

The process then continues with x_2 which gives us the next integer n_3 and so on. Stopping the process at any point will provide a rational approximation for x. As an example table 5 shows rational approximations for the base 2 logarithm of 3 which is equal to $\log_2(3) = 1.584962500721156\ldots$.

rational approx.	floating point
3/2	1.5
8/5	1.6
19/12	$1.58\overline{3}$
65/41	$1.\overline{58536}$
84/53	1.584905660377
485/306	1.584967320261

Table 5: Rational approximations for the base 2 logarithm of 3.

REVIEW OF DISCRETE PROBABILITY

Discrete probability is concerned with observations, experiments or actions that have a finite or countably infinite number of unpredictable outcomes. Countably infinite means the outcomes can be counted or labeled by the natural numbers, $1, 2, 3, \ldots$. The set of all possible outcomes is called the sample space (standard terminology) and is denoted by the symbol Ω. An element of Ω (an individual outcome) will be denoted by ω. A coin toss for example, has two possible outcomes: heads (H) or tails (T). The sample space is $\Omega = \{H, T\}$ and $\omega = H$ is one of the possible outcomes. Another example is the roll of a die which has 6 outcomes so that $\Omega = \{1, 2, 3, 4, 5, 6\}$. A subset of the sample space is called an event and is denoted by a capital letter such as A or B. In the die example, let A be the event that an even number is rolled, then $A = \{2, 4, 6\}$.

Each outcome, ω, has a probability assigned to it, denoted $P(\omega)$. The probability is a real number ranging from 0 to 1 that signifies the likelihood that an outcome will occur. If $P(\omega) = 0$ then ω will never occur and if $P(\omega) = 1$ then ω will always occur. An intermediate value such as $P(\omega) = 1/2$ means that ω will occur roughly half the time if the experiment is repeated many times. In general, if you perform the experiment a large number of times, N, and the number of times that ω occurs is $n(\omega)$, then the ratio $n(\omega)/N$ should approximately equal the probability of ω. It is possible to define $P(\omega)$ as the limit of this ratio.

$$P(\omega) = \lim_{N \to \infty} \frac{n(\omega)}{N} \tag{87}$$

In other words, if you could repeat the experiment an infinite number of times, the fraction of the time that the outcome is ω, is the probability of ω.

The function $P(\omega)$, which assigns probabilities to outcomes, is called a probability distribution. We will now look at some of its properties. To begin with, if the probabilities are defined as in equation 87, then clearly the sum of all probabilities must equal 1.

$$\sum_{\omega \in \Omega} P(\omega) = 1 \tag{88}$$

It is often necessary to determine the probability that one of a subset of all the possible outcomes will occur. If A is a subset of Ω then $P(A)$ is the probability that one of the outcomes contained in A will occur. Using the definition in 87 it should be obvious that:

$$P(A) = \sum_{\omega \in A} P(\omega) \tag{89}$$

Many other properties can be derived from the algebra of sets. Let $A + B$ be the set of all elements in either A or B (no duplicates) and let AB be the the set of all elements in both A and B, then:

$$P(A + B) = P(A) + P(B) - P(AB) \tag{90}$$

If A and B have no elements in common then they are exclusive events, i.e. they can not both occur simultaneously. In this case equation 90 reduces to $P(A+B) = P(A) + P(B)$. In general, the probability that any one of a number of exclusive events will occur is just equal to the sum of their individual probabilities.

Conditional probabilities and the closely related concept of independence are very important and useful in probability calculations. Let $P(A|B)$ be the probability that A has occurred given that we know B has occurred. In short, we will refer to this as the probability of A given B or the probability of A conditioned on B. What $P(A|B)$ really represents is the probability of A using B as the sample space instead of Ω. If A and

B have no elements in common then $P(A|B) = 0$. If they have all elements in common so that $A = B$ then obviously $P(A|B) = 1$. If A is a subset of B, meaning that every element of A is also an element of B, then $P(A|B) = P(A)/P(B)$. In the general case we have:

$$P(A|B) = \frac{P(AB)}{P(B)} \tag{91}$$

Using a single fair die roll as an example, let $A = \{1,3\}$ and $B = \{3,5\}$ then $AB = \{3\}$, $P(AB) = 1/6$, $P(B) = 1/3$ and

$$P(A|B) = \frac{1/6}{1/3} = \frac{1}{2} \tag{92}$$

Knowledge that B has occurred has increased the probability of A from $P(A) = 1/3$ to $P(A|B) = 1/2$. The result can also be deduced by simple logic. We know that B has occurred, therefore the roll was either a 3 or a 5. Half of the B events are caused by a 3 and half by a 5 but only the 3 counts as an A event, therefore $P(A|B) = 1/2$.

Conditional probabilities are not necessarily symmetric. $P(B|A)$ need not be equal to $P(A|B)$. Using the definition in equation 91, you can show that

$$P(A|B)P(B) = P(B|A)P(A) \tag{93}$$

so the two conditional probabilities are only equal if $P(A) = P(B)$. Another useful thing to keep in mind is that conditional probabilities obey the same properties as non-conditional probabilities. This means for example that if A and B are exclusive events then $P(A + B|C) = P(A|C) + P(B|C)$.

The concept of independence is naturally related to conditional probability. Two events are independent if the occurrence of one has no effect on the probability of the other. In terms of conditional probabilities this means that $P(A|B) = P(A)$. Independence is always symmetric, if A is independent of B then B is independent of A. Using the definition in equation 91 you can see that independence also implies that

$$P(AB) = P(A)P(B) \tag{94}$$

This is often taken as the defining relation for independence.

Another important concept in probability is the law of total probability. Let the sample space Ω be partitioned by the sets B_1 and B_2 so that every element in

Ω is in one and only one of the two sets and we can write $\Omega = B_1 + B_2$. This means that the occurrence of A coincides with the occurrence of B_1 or B_2 but not both and we can write

$$A = AB_1 + AB_2 = A(B_1 + B_2) = A\Omega \tag{95}$$

The probability of A is then

$$P(A) = P(AB_1) + P(AB_2) \tag{96}$$

This can be extended to any number of sets that partition Ω.

Doing any kind of probabilistic analysis usually requires random variables. A random variable is a bit like the probability distributions discussed above in that it assigns a number to each of the elements in the sample space. It is therefore really more like a function that maps elements in the sample space to real numbers. A random variable is usually denoted with an upper case letter such as X and the values it can assume are given subscripted lower case letters such as x_i for $i = 1, 2, \ldots, n$ where n is the number of possible values. The mapping from an element ω to a value x_i is denoted as $X(\omega) = x_i$. Note that it is not necessary that every element be assigned a unique value and the particular value assigned will depend on what you want to analyze.

A simple example is a coin toss betting game. You guess what the result of the toss will be. If your guess is correct you win \$1 otherwise you lose \$1. The sample space consists of only two elements, a correct guess and an incorrect guess $\Omega = \{\text{correct}, \text{incorrect}\}$. If you are interested in analyzing the amounts won and lost by playing several such games then the obvious choice for the random variable is $X(\text{correct}) = 1$, $X(\text{incorrect}) = -1$. If you are just interested in the number of games won or lost then the random variable $Y(\text{correct}) = 1$, $Y(\text{incorrect}) = 0$ would be better. Often an analysis in terms of one variable can be converted into another variable by finding a relation between them. In the above example $X = 2Y - 1$ could be used to convert between the variables.

As another example consider tossing a coin three times. The sample space consists of 8 elements
$$\Omega = \{TTT, TTH, THT, THH, HTT, HTH, HHT, HHH\}$$
where T indicates the toss was a tail and H a head. This time we let X be the random variable that counts the number of heads in the three tosses. It can have values 0, 1, 2, or 3 and not every element in the sample space has a unique value. The values are $X(TTT) = 0$, $X(TTH) = X(THT) = X(HTT) = 1$, $X(THH) = X(HTH) = X(HHT) = 2$, $X(HHH) = 3$.

Probability distributions are most often expressed in terms of the values that a random variable can take. The usual notation is

$$P(X = x_i) = p(x_i) \tag{97}$$

The function $p(x_i)$ is the probability distribution for the random variable X. It is often also called the probability mass function. Note that it is not necessarily the same as the probability distribution for the individual elements of the sample space since multiple elements may be mapped to the same value by the random variable. In the three coin toss example, each element in the sample space has a probability of 1/8, assuming a fair coin. The probability distribution for X however is $p(0) = 1/8$, $p(1) = 3/8$, $p(2) = 3/8$, $p(3) = 1/8$. It will always be true that the sum over all the probabilities must equal 1.

$$\sum_i p(x_i) = 1 \tag{98}$$

The two most important properties of a random variable are its expectation (also called mean) and variance. The expectation is simply the average value of the random variable. In the coin toss betting game, X can have a value of +1 or -1 corresponding to winning or losing. In N flips of the coin let k be the number of wins and $N-k$ the number of losses. The total amount won is then

$$W = k - (N - k) \tag{99}$$

and the average amount won per flip is

$$\frac{W}{N} = \frac{k}{N} - (1 - \frac{k}{N}) \tag{100}$$

As the number of flips becomes very large the ratio k/N will equal $p(1)$, the probability of winning, and the equation then becomes equal to the expectation of the random variable.

$$E[X] = p(1) - p(-1) \tag{101}$$

Where $p(-1) = 1 - p(1)$ is the probability of losing and $E[X]$ is the usual notation for the expectation of X. In this case the expectation is the average amount that you can expect to win per flip if you play the game for a very long time.

In general if X can take on n values, x_i, $i = 1, 2, \ldots, n$

with corresponding probabilities $p(x_i)$ then the expectation is

$$E[X] = \sum_{i=1}^{n} p(x_i)x_i \tag{102}$$

The expectation gives you the average, but in reality large deviations from the average may be possible. The variance of a random variable gives a sense for how large those deviations can be. It measures the average of the squares of the deviations. The equation for the variance is:

$$\text{Var}[X] = \sum_{i=1}^{n} p(x_i)(x_i - E[X])^2 \tag{103}$$

The equation simplifies somewhat to

$$\text{Var}[X] = E[X^2] - E[X]^2 \tag{104}$$

where

$$E[X^2] = \sum_{i=1}^{n} p(x_i)x_i^2 \tag{105}$$

is the expectation for the square of the random variable. In general the expectation for any function, $g(X)$, of the random variable is:

$$E[g(X)] = \sum_{i=1}^{n} p(x_i)g(x_i) \qquad (106)$$

Another useful measure of deviation from the average is called the standard deviation, σ. It is found by taking the square root of the variance.

$$\sigma = \sqrt{\mathrm{Var}[X]} \qquad (107)$$

As we saw above, a sample space can have more than one random variable defined on it. If we have two variables X and Y then we can define the probability that $X = x_i$ at the same time that $Y = y_j$. This is called the joint probability distribution for X and Y.

$$P(X = x_i, Y = y_j) = p(x_i, y_j) \qquad (108)$$

The individual distributions, $p(x_i)$ and $p(y_j)$, are recovered by summing the joint distribution over one of the variables. To get $p(x_i)$ you sum $p(x_i, y_j)$ over all the possible values of Y.

$$p(x_i) = \sum_j p(x_i, y_j) \tag{109}$$

and likewise for $p(y_j)$

$$p(y_j) = \sum_i p(x_i, y_j) \tag{110}$$

From these last two equations it is obvious that if you sum over both variables of the distribution, the result should equal 1.

$$\sum_i \sum_j p(x_i, y_j) = 1 \tag{111}$$

It is possible to construct a joint distribution for any number of random variables, not just 2. For example $p(x_i, y_j, z_k)$ would be a joint distribution for the variables X, Y, and Z.

With a joint distribution you can calculate the expectation and variance for functions of variables. The expectation for the sum $X + Y$ is:

$$\begin{aligned}
E[X+Y] &= \sum_i \sum_j p(x_i, y_j)(x_i + y_j) \qquad (112)\\
&= \sum_i x_i \sum_j p(x_i, y_j) + \sum_j y_j \sum_i p(x_i, y_j)\\
&= \sum_i x_i p(x_i) + \sum_j y_j p(y_j)\\
&= E[X] + E[Y]
\end{aligned}$$

The property that the expectation for a sum of variables is equal to the sum of their expectations is called linearity and it is true for the sum of any number of variables. For three variables for example $E[X + Y + Z] = E[X] + E[Y] + E[Z]$. Another easily verifiable consequence of linearity is that for any constants a and b

$$E[aX + bY] = aE[X] + bE[Y] \qquad (113)$$

In the example of the coin toss game we had two random variables that were related by $X = 2Y - 1$. The linearity property of the expectation means that $E[X] = 2E[Y] - 1$, where we used the fact that the expectation of a constant is just the constant.

The expectation for the product XY is

$$E[XY] = \sum_i \sum_j p(x_i, y_j) x_i y_j \tag{114}$$

If the variables X and Y are independent then the joint distribution can be factored into a product of the individual distributions, $p(x_i, y_j) = p(x_i)p(y_j)$. In this case you can show that the expectation of the product is the product of the expectations, $E[XY] = E[X]E[Y]$.

For the variance of a sum we have

$$\text{Var}[X + Y] = E[(X - E[X] + Y - E[Y])^2] \tag{115}$$

after expanding and simplifying this becomes

$$\text{Var}[X + Y] = \text{Var}[X] + \text{Var}[Y] + 2\text{Cov}[X, Y] \tag{116}$$

where $\text{Cov}[X, Y]$ is called the covariance of X and Y. The covariance is defined as:

$$\text{Cov}[X, Y] = E[XY] - E[X]E[Y] \tag{117}$$

For independent variables the covariance is zero. The variance of the sum is then just the sum of the variances.

That completes our review of discrete probability.

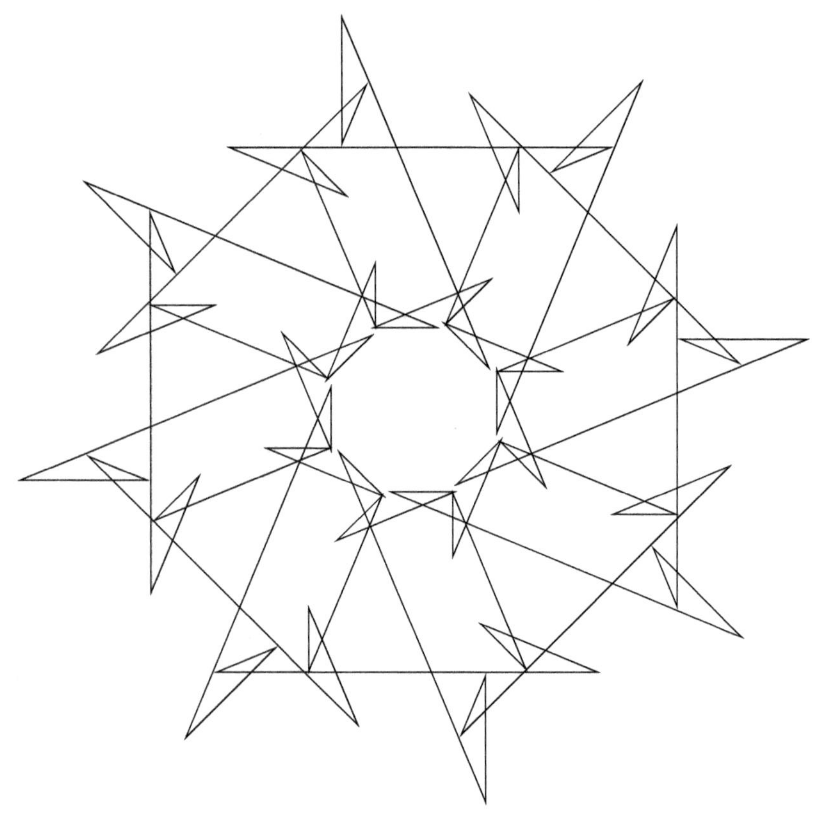

REFERENCES & FURTHER READING

- *Elements of Information Theory*, 2nd edition, Cover and Thomas, 2006.

- *Information Theory and Reliable Communication*, Robert G. Gallager, 1968.

- *The Information: a History, a Theory, a Flood*, James Gleick, 2011.

- *Bet Smart: The Kelly System for Gambling and Investing*, Hollos and Hollos, 2008.

- *Fundamentals of Error-Correcting Codes*, Huffman and Pless, 2003.

- *The Theory of Error-Correcting Codes*, MacWilliams and Sloane, 1977.

- *An Introduction to Information Theory: Symbols, Signals & Noise*, 2nd rev. edition, John R. Pierce, 1980.

- *Fortune's Formula: The Untold Story of the Scientific Betting System that Beat the Casinos and Wall Street*, William Poundstone, 2005.

- *A Diary on Information Theory*, Alfred Renyi, 1987.

- *The Mathematical Theory of Communication*, Shannon and Weaver, 1949.

- *Claude Elwood Shannon (1916-2001)*, Golomb, Berlekamp, Cover, Massey and Viterbi, Notices of the AMS, Vol 49, No 1, January 2002, p8-16. http://www.ams.org/notices/200201/

- *Coin-Weighing Problems*, Richard K. Guy and Richard J. Nowakowski, American Mathematical Monthly, Vol 102, No 2, Feb 1995, p164-167.

- *Error Detecting and Error Correcting Codes*, Richard W. Hamming, Bell System Technical Journal, Vol 29, No 2, 1950, p147-160.

- *A Method for the Construction of Minimum-Redundancy Codes*, David A. Huffman, Proceedings of the IRE, Vol 40, No 9, September 1952, p1098-1102.

- *Information Theory and Statistical Mechanics*, Edwin T. Jaynes, Physical Review, Vol 106, No 4, May 15 1957, p620-630.

- *Arithmetic Coding Revisited*, Moffat, Neal and Witten, ACM Transactions on Information Systems, Vol 16, 1995, p256-294.

- *Searching Games with Errors - Fifty Years of Coping with Liars*, Andrzej Pelc, Theoretical Computer Science, Vol 270, No 1-2, Jan 2002, p71-109.

- *A Logarithm Algorithm*, Daniel Shanks, Mathematics of Computation, Vol 8, No 46, 1954, p60-64.

- *Prediction and Entropy of Printed English*, Claude E. Shannon, Bell System Technical Journal, Vol 30, No 1, 1951, p50-64.

- *Fifty Years of Shannon Theory*, Sergio Verdu, IEEE Transactions on Information Theory, Vol 44, No 6, October 1998, p2057-2078.

- *Arithmetic Coding for Data Compression*, Witten, Neal and Cleary, Communications of the ACM, Vol 30, 1987, p520-540.

- *English Letter Frequency Counts: Mayzner Revisited or ETAOIN SRHLDCU*, Peter Norvig. http://norvig.com/mayzner.html

- *Mathematical Theory of Claude Shannon*, Chiu, Lin, Mcferron, Petigara and Seshasai. http://web.mit.edu/6.933/www/Fall2001/Shannon1.pdf

- C language software for arithmetic coding can be found at Radford Neal's webpage: http://www.cs.toronto.edu/ radford/ac.software.html

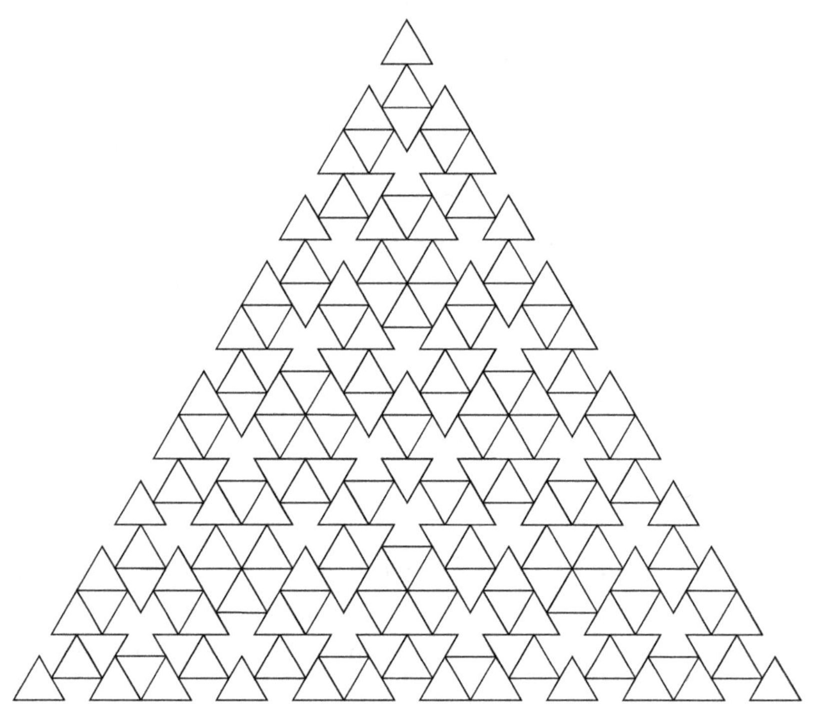

ACKNOWLEDGMENTS

In ordinary life we hardly realize that we receive a great deal more than we give, and that it is only with gratitude that life becomes rich. It is very easy to overestimate the importance of our own achievements in comparison with what we owe to others.

Dietrich Bonhoeffer, letter to parents from prison, Sept. 13, 1943

We'd like to thank our parents, Istvan and Anna Hollos, for helping us in many ways.

We thank the makers and maintainers of all the software we've used in the production of this book, including: the Emacs text editor, the LaTeX typesetting system, Inkscape, asymptote language, mupdf and evince document viewers, Maxima computer algebra system, gcc, awk, bash shell, and the GNU/Linux operating system.

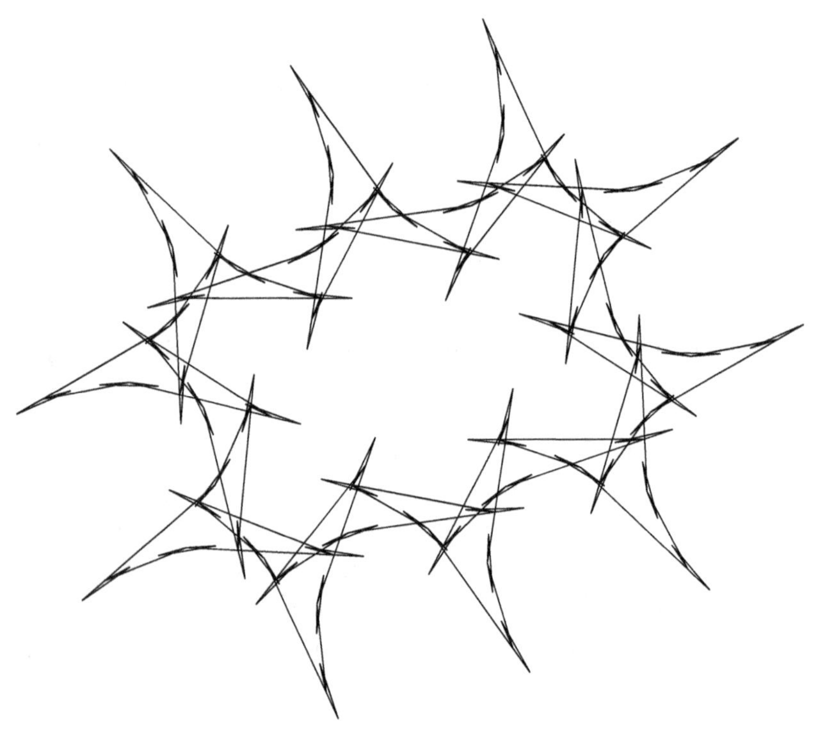

ABOUT THE AUTHORS

Stefan Hollos and **J. Richard Hollos** are physicists by training, and enjoy anything related to math, physics, and computing. They are the authors of

- **Recursive Digital Filters: A Concise Guide**

- **Art of Pi**

- **Creating Noise**

- **Art of the Golden Ratio**

- **Creating Rhythms**

- **Pattern Generation for Computational Art**

- **Finite Automata and Regular Expressions: Problems and Solutions**

- **Probability Problems and Solutions**

- **Combinatorics Problems and Solutions**

- **The Coin Toss: Probabilities and Patterns**

- **Pairs Trading: A Bayesian Example**

- **Simple Trading Strategies That Work**

- **Bet Smart: The Kelly System for Gambling and Investing**

- **Signals from the Subatomic World: How to Build a Proton Precession Magnetometer**

They are brothers and business partners at Exstrom Laboratories LLC in Longmont, Colorado. Their website is exstrom.com

THANK YOU

Thank you for buying this book.

Sign up for the Abrazol Publishing Newsletter and receive news on new editions, new products, and special offers. Just go to

http://www.abrazol.com/

and enter your email address.

www.ingramcontent.com/pod-product-compliance
Lightning Source LLC
Chambersburg PA
CBHW060937050726
47592CB00003B/987